OCS EIS/EA
MMS 2004-068

Environmental Assessment

Proposed OCS Lease Sale 194, Central Gulf of Mexico

I0428109

Author

Minerals Management Service
Gulf of Mexico OCS Region

U.S. Department of the Interior
Minerals Management Service
Gulf of Mexico OCS Region

New Orleans
November 2004

FINDING OF NO NEW SIGNIFICANT IMPACT

The U.S. Department of the Interior, Minerals Management Service (MMS) has prepared an environmental assessment (EA) for proposed Lease Sale 194 in the Central Planning Area (CPA) of the Gulf of Mexico (GOM) Outer Continental Shelf (OCS) to determine whether MMS can make a Finding of No New Significant Impact (FONNSI) or should prepare a supplemental environmental impact statement (EIS). In November 2002, MMS filed with the U.S. Environmental Protection Agency a Final EIS covering CPA Lease Sales 185, 190, 194, 198, and 201; and Western Planning Area Lease Sales 187, 192, 196, and 200 in the GOM (multisale EIS). Because the multisale EIS examined the environmental impacts of a sale similar in size, nature, and potential level of development as Lease Sale 194, this EA tiers off the multisale EIS and incorporates much of the material by reference. It also reexamines the potential environmental effects of the proposed action and alternatives based on any new information regarding potential impacts or issues that were not available at the time the multisale EIS was prepared.

The purpose of the EA is to analyze whether new information indicates that there are likely to be significant new impacts that were not addressed in the multisale EIS. As part of the scoping process for the EA, MMS reviewed new information to determine if any resources should be reevaluated or if the new information would alter conclusions of the multisale EIS. It was determined that four resources (marine mammals, sea turtles, Gulf sturgeon, and snowy plover) should be reevaluated because of new information. The new information for these four resources (mitigation measures for protected species, designation of critical habitat for the Gulf sturgeon, a revised oil-spill probability for the snow plover) is analyzed in the EA.

The EA also presents a study of the impacts of Hurricane Lili, updates of MMS's preparation of National Environmental Policy Act documents for seismic surveys and structure removal operations, more exact estimates of the abundance of cetaceans in the northern GOM, proposed liquefied natural gas projects, proposed sand dredging projects, and additional scoping opportunities since the multisale EIS. This new information further supports or elaborates on analyses or information presented in the multisale EIS, but it does not change any of the analyses in the multisale EIS.

Based on the analyses in the EA, no new significant impacts were identified for proposed Lease Sale 194 that were not already assessed in the multisale EIS, nor is it necessary to change the conclusions of the kinds, levels, or locations of impacts described in that document. Therefore, MMS has determined that a supplemental EIS is not required and is issuing this FONNSI.

Supporting Documents

Proposed OCS Lease Sale 194, Central Gulf of Mexico—Environmental Assessment (USDOI, MMS, 2004) (attached).

Gulf of Mexico OCS Oil and Gas Lease Sales: 2003-2007; Central Planning Area Sales 185, 190, 194, 198, and 201; Western Planning Area Sales 187, 192, 196, and 200—Final Environmental Impact Statement; Volumes I and II (USDOI, MMS, 2002) (available upon request).

_____   _____
              Director   11 - 1 - 04
                                                     Date

TABLE OF CONTENTS

FIGURES

TABLES

ABBREVIATIONS AND ACRONYMS

5-Year Program	*Outer Continental Shelf Oil and Gas Leasing Program 2002-2007*	MMPA	Marine Mammal Protection Act of 1972
ADCP	Acoustic Doppler Current Profile	MMS	Minerals Management Service
bbl	barrel	MODU	mobile offshore drilling unit
BBO	billion barrels of oil	NEPA	National Environmental Policy Act
BML	below mud line	NOAA	National Oceanic and Atmospheric Administration
BO	Biological Opinion		
Btu	British thermal unit		
Call	Call for Information and Nominations	NOI	Notice of Intent to Prepare an EIS
CD	Consistency Determination	NO_x	nitrogen oxide
COE	United States Army Corps of Engineers	NPDES	National Pollution Discharge Elimination System
CPA	Central Planning Area	NTL	Notice to Lessees and Operators
CWPPRA	Coastal Wetlands Planning, Protection, and Restoration Act	OCS	Outer Continental Shelf
		OSRA	Oil-Spill Risk Analysis
CZM	Coastal Zone Management	PEA	Programmatic Environmental Assessment
DWPA	Deepwater Ports Act		
EA	Environmental Assessment	PEIS	Programmatic EIS
EFH	essential fish habitat	PM_{10}	particulate matter smaller than 10 microns
EIS	Environmental Impact Statement		
		ROV	remotely operated vehicle
EPA	Eastern Planning Area	SBF	synthetic-based drilling fluids
ESA	Endangered Species Act of 1973	Secretary	Secretary of the Interior
		SO_x	sulphur oxide
FONSI	Finding of No Significant Impact	SWAMP	Sperm Whale Acoustic Monitoring Program
FWS	U.S. Fish and Wildlife Service	SWSS	Sperm Whale Seismic Survey
		TAOS	Technical Assessment and Operation Support
G&G	geological and geophysical		
GBS	gravity-based structure	Tcf	trillion cubic feet
GOM	Gulf of Mexico	USCG	United States Coast Guard
ITS	Incidental Take Statement	USDOI	United States Department of the Interior
LARI	Louisiana Artificial Reef Initiative		
LCA	Louisiana Coastal Area	USDOT	United States Department of Transportation
LDWF	Louisiana Department of Wildlife and Fisheries	USEPA	United States Environmental Protection Agency
LNG	liquefied natural gas	WPA	Western Planning Area
MARAD	Maritime Administration		

1. OBJECTIVES OF THE ENVIRONMENTAL ASSESSMENT

This environmental assessment (EA) addresses one proposed Federal action: oil and gas Lease Sale 194 in the proposed lease sale area of the Central Planning Area (CPA) of the Gulf of Mexico (GOM) Outer Continental Shelf (OCS) as scheduled in the *Outer Continental Shelf Oil and Gas Leasing Program 2002-2007* (5-Year Program) (USDOI, MMS, 2002a). This EA incorporates by reference all of the relevant material in the multisale environmental impact statement (EIS) from which it tiers (*Gulf of Mexico OCS Oil and Gas Lease Sales: 2003-2007; Central Planning Area Sales 185, 190, 194, 198, and 201; Western Planning Area Sales 187, 192, 196, and 200; Final Environmental Impact Statement; Volumes I and II* (USDOI, MMS, 2002b)). The EA has been prepared to aid in the determination of whether or not new available information indicates that the proposed lease sale would result in new significant impacts not addressed in the multisale EIS.

In preparation for this EA, the U.S. Department of the Interior (USDOI) Minerals Management Service (MMS) reexamined the potential environmental effects of the proposed action and the alternatives based on any new information regarding potential impacts and issues not available at the time MMS prepared the multisale EIS in November 2002. New information was reviewed to determine if any resources should be reevaluated or if the new information would alter conclusions of the multisale EIS. It was determined that four resources (marine mammals, sea turtles, Gulf sturgeon, and snowy plover) should be reevaluated because of new information. The new information for these four resources is the mitigation measures for protected species, the designation of critical habitat for the Gulf sturgeon, and a revised oil-spill probability for the snow plover.

Federal regulations allow for an agency to analyze related or similar proposals in one EIS (40 CFR 1502.4). Since the CPA Lease Sales 185, 190, 194, 198, and 201 and their projected activities are very similar, if not almost identical, MMS prepared a single EIS for the five lease sales. The multisale approach focuses the National Environmental Policy Act (NEPA) EIS process on the differences between the proposed lease sales and new information and issues. Although the multisale EIS addressed five proposed CPA lease sale actions, the Secretary of the Interior (Secretary) makes a separate decision for each lease sale.

The multisale EIS can be obtained from the Minerals Management Service, Gulf of Mexico OCS Region, Attention: Public Information Office (MS 5034), 1201 Elmwood Park Boulevard, Room 114, New Orleans, Louisiana 70123-2394 (1-800-200-GULF) or viewed on the MMS website at http://www.gomr.mms.gov. A list of libraries that have copies of the multisale EIS and their locations is also available on the MMS Internet website.

2. PURPOSE OF AND NEED FOR THE PROPOSED ACTION

Purpose of the Proposed Action

The purpose of this proposed action (CPA Lease Sale 194) is to offer for lease all unleased blocks in the proposed lease sale area (**Figure 1**) that may contain economically recoverable oil and natural gas resources. The proposed lease sale would provide qualified bidders the opportunity to bid upon and lease acreage in the proposed lease sale area in order to explore, develop, and produce oil and natural gas.

Need for the Proposed Action

The Central GOM constitutes one of the world's major oil- and gas-producing areas and has proved to be a steady and reliable source of crude oil and natural gas for more than 50 years. Oil from the GOM would help reduce the Nation's need for oil imports and reduce the environmental risks associated with oil tankering. Natural gas is generally considered to be an environmentally preferable alternative to oil in terms of both production and consumption.

3.   ALTERNATIVES INCLUDING THE PROPOSED ACTION

3.1.   ALTERNATIVE A—PROPOSED ACTION

Alternative A—The Proposed Action: Under proposed CPA Lease Sale 194, MMS would offer for lease all unleased blocks within the CPA for oil and natural gas operations, with the following exceptions: Lund South (Area NG16-07) Blocks 172, 173, 213-217, 252-261, 296-305, and 349; Amery Terrace (Area NG15-09) Blocks 280, 281, 318-320, and 355-359; and portions of Amery Terrace (Area NG15-09) Blocks 235-238, 273-279, and 309-359, which are deferred from the proposed action under the "Treaty Between the Government of the United States of America and the Government of the United Mexican States on the Delimitation Of The Continental Shelf in the Western Gulf of Mexico Beyond 200 Nautical Miles." The CPA encompasses about 47.8 million ac in water depths ranging from 4 to 3,400 m **(Figure 1)**. The estimated amount of resources projected to be developed as a result of proposed CPA Lease Sale 194 is 0.276-0.654 billion barrels of oil (BBO) and 1.590-3.300 trillion cubic feet (Tcf) of natural gas.

In the multisale EIS, a proposed action is presented as a set of ranges for resource estimates, projected exploration and development activities, and impact-producing factors. All of the proposed CPA lease sales analyzed in the multisale EIS is expected to be within the scenario ranges presented for a typical CPA lease sale; therefore, a proposed action is representative of each proposed lease sale.

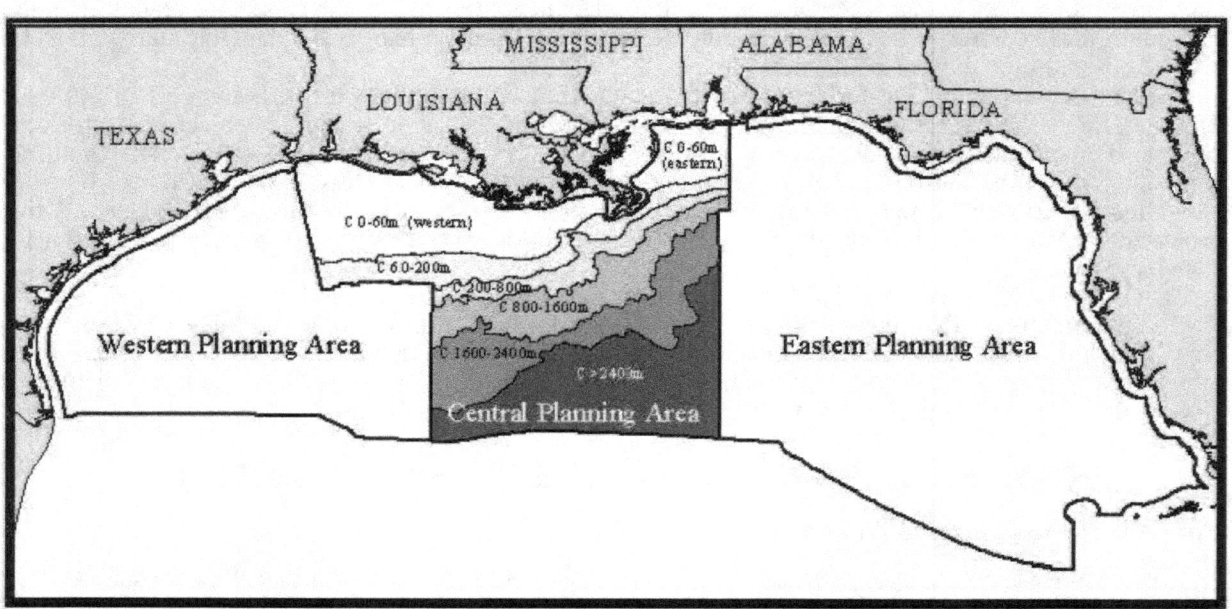

Figure 1.   GOM OCS Planning Areas and CPA Offshore Subareas.

3.2.   ALTERNATIVES TO THE PROPOSED ACTION

Alternative B — The Proposed Action Excluding the Unleased Blocks Near Biologically Sensitive Topographic Features: This alternative would offer for lease all unleased blocks in the CPA, as described for the proposed action, with the exception of any unleased blocks within the 167 blocks subject to the Topographic Features Stipulation.

Alternative C — The Proposed Action Excluding the Unleased Blocks Within 15 Miles of the Baldwin County, Alabama, Coast: This alternative would offer for lease all unleased blocks in the CPA, as described for the proposed action, with the exception of any unleased blocks within 15 mi of the Baldwin County, Alabama, coast.

Alternative D — No Action: This alternative is equivalent to the cancellation of the proposed CPA Lease Sale 194. The opportunity for development of the estimated 0.276-0.654 BBO oil and 1.590-3.300 Tcf of natural gas resources that could have resulted from the proposed action would be precluded or postponed. Any potential environmental impacts resulting from the proposed action would not occur or would be postponed.

3.3. MITIGATION MEASURES

The proposed action and all subsequent activities resulting from it are subject to the existing regulations and proposed lease stipulations designed to reduce environmental risks. Lease stipulations are legally binding restrictions and operating requirements that are made a part of every oil and gas lease document. Six stipulations will be applied to leases resulting from CPA Lease Sale 194 as and if appropriate. Five of the stipulations (Topographic Features; Live Bottom (Pinnacle Trend); Military Areas; Blocks South of Baldwin County, Alabama; and Law of the Sea Convention Royalty Payment Stipulations) are included in the multisale EIS. **Chapter 2.3.1.3.** of the multisale EIS discusses the effectiveness of these stipulations.

Following the completion of the multisale EIS, an additional stipulation, Protected Species, was adopted for CPA Lease Sale 185 (March 2003), which was the first CPA lease sale held under the multisale EIS. Its requirements, which are described below in **Chapter 3.3.1.**, also apply to CPA Lease Sale 194. The Protected Species Stipulation was developed in consultation with the National Oceanic and Atmospheric Administration (NOAA) and the U.S. Fish and Wildlife Service (FWS). A seventh stipulation is in development and will be recommended to apply to portions of Vermilion Blocks 139 and 140 that are involved with approved liquefied natural gas (LNG) projects. Instead of deferring these blocks, all exploration, development, and production activities or operations must take place from outside the lease by the use of directional drilling or other techniques.

The MMS has also issued 35 Notices to Lessees and Operators (NTL) since the completion of the multisale EIS in order to

- clarify, describe, or interpret regulation or OCS standards;

- provide guidelines on the implementation of a special lease stipulation or regional requirement;

- provide a better understanding of the scope and meaning of a regulation by explaining MMS interpretation of a requirement; or

- transmit administrative information.

A list of the new NTL's can be found in **Appendix A**, while the actual NTL's are on the MMS Internet website at www.gomr.mms.gov/homepg/regulate/regs/ntls/ntl_1st.html. The requirements addressed in these NTL's apply to all existing and future oil and natural gas operations on the GOM OCS. Five of the new NTL's (Vessel Strike Avoidance and Injured/Dead Protected Species Reporting; Marine Trash and Debris Awareness and Elimination; Implementation of Seismic Survey Mitigation Measures and Protected Species Observer Program; Biologically Sensitive Areas of the Gulf of Mexico; and Structure-Removal Operations) and the proposed Deepwater Ocean Current Monitoring on Floating Facilities NTL are discussed in **Chapter 3.3.2.**

3.3.1. Protected Species Stipulation

The Protected Species Stipulation is designed to minimize or avoid potential adverse impacts to federally protected species (e.g., sea turtles, marine mammals, Gulf sturgeon, and other listed species). To reduce the potential taking of federally protected species

(1) The MMS conditions all permits issued to lessees and their operators to require them to collect and remove flotsam resulting from activities related to exploration, development, and production of this lease.

(2) The MMS conditions all permits issued to lessees and their operators to require them to post signs in prominent places on all vessels and platforms used as a result of

activities related to exploration, development, and production of this lease detailing the reasons (legal and ecological) why the release of debris must be eliminated.

(3) The MMS requires that vessel operators and crews watch for marine mammals and sea turtles, reduce vessel speed to 10 kt or less when assemblages of cetaceans are observed, and maintain a distance of 90 m or greater from whales and a distance of 45 m or greater from small cetaceans and sea turtles.

(4) The MMS requires that all seismic surveys employ mandatory mitigation measures including the use of a 500-m "exclusion zone" based upon the appropriate water depth, ramp-up and shut-down procedures, visual monitoring, and reporting. Seismic operations must immediately cease when whales are detected within the 500-m exclusion zone. Ramp-up procedures and seismic surveys may be initiated only during daylight unless alternate monitoring methods approved by MMS are used.

(5) The MMS requires lessees and operators to instruct offshore personnel to immediately report all sightings and locations of injured or dead protected species (marine mammals and sea turtles) to the appropriate stranding network. If oil and gas industry activity is responsible for the injured or dead animals (e.g., because of a vessel strike), the responsible parties should remain available to assist the stranding network. If the injury or death is caused by a vessel collision, the responsible party must notify MMS within 24 hours of the strike.

(6) The MMS requires oil-spill contingency planning to identify important habitats, including designated critical habitat, used by listed species (e.g., sea turtle nesting beaches, and piping plover critical habitat) and will require the strategic placement of spill cleanup equipment to be used only by personnel trained in less intrusive cleanup techniques on beach and bay shores.

The analyses of potential proposed action impacts to marine mammals, sea turtles, Gulf sturgeon, and snowy plover are presented in **Chapter 4.2.** of this EA.

3.3.2. Notices to Lessees and Operators

Vessel Strike Avoidance and Injured/Dead Protected Species Reporting (NTL 2003-G10)

The Vessel Strike Avoidance and Injured/Dead Protected Species Reporting NTL (NTL 2003-G10) provides the following guidelines to minimize the risk of vessel strikes to protected species and report observations of injured or dead protected species.

Protected Species Identification Training

Vessel crews are to use a GOM reference guide to identify marine mammals and sea turtles.

Vessel Strike Avoidance

The following guidelines are included:

(1) Vessel operators and crews should maintain a vigilant watch for marine mammals and sea turtles and slow down or stop their vessels to avoid striking protected species.

(2) When a whale is sighted, a distance of 90 m or greater from the whale should be maintained.

(3) When sea turtles or small cetaceans are sighted, there should be an attempt to maintain a distance of 45 m or greater whenever possible.

(4) When cetaceans are sighted while a vessel is underway, there should be an attempt to remain parallel to the animals' course. Excessive speed or abrupt changes in direction until the cetaceans have left the area should be avoided.

(5) Vessel speed should be reduced to 10 kt or less when pods or large assemblages of cetaceans are observed near an underway vessel. Cetaceans at the surface may indicate the presence of submerged animals near the vessel.

(6) Whales may surface in unpredictable locations or approach slowly moving vessels. When animals are sighted in the vessel's path or in close proximity to a moving vessel, speed should be reduced and the engine shifted to neutral. Engines should not be engaged until the animals are clear of the area.

Injured/Dead Protected Species Reporting

Vessel crews must report sightings of any injured or dead protected species (marine mammals and sea turtles) immediately to the Marine Mammal and Sea Turtle Stranding Hotline or the Marine Mammal Stranding Network. If oil and gas industry activity is responsible for the injury or death of a protected species, MMS must be notified within 24 hours and the responsible parties should remain available to assist the respective salvage and stranding network as needed.

Marine Trash and Debris Awareness and Elimination (NTL 2003-G11)

The Marine Trash and Debris Awareness and Elimination NTL (NTL 2003-G11) provides guidance to reduce the accidental introduction of marine trash and debris into the GOM. This NTL requires the placement of marine debris elimination placards, with specified language, in prominent places on all fixed and floating production facilities that have sleeping or food preparation capabilities, and on all mobile drilling units engaged in oil and gas operations in the GOM OCS. This NTL also requires marine debris awareness training for all offshore employees and contractors actively engaged in offshore operations. This training includes viewing a training video or slide show and receiving an explanation from the company's management that emphasizes their commitment to achieve the objectives of the trash and debris containment requirement. This NTL describes certification guidelines including the preparation of an annual report to MMS from a company official that describes the marine trash and debris awareness training process and certifies that the training process has been followed for the previous calendar year.

Implementation of Seismic Survey Mitigation Measures and Protected Species Observer Program (NTL 2004-G01)

The MMS superseded NTL 2003-G08, Implementation of Seismic Survey Mitigation Measures and Protected Species Observer Program, with NTL 2004-G01. The new NTL, which expands application of the seismic survey mitigation measures to include additional marine mammal species, became effective March 1, 2004.

The Implementation of Seismic Survey Mitigation Measures and Protected Species Observer Program NTL (NTL 2004-G01) details information on ramp-up procedures, observation methods, and reporting requirements to be followed by the seismic industry during certain geological and geophysical (G&G) survey operations. The conditions prescribed under this NTL aid in reducing the chance of harassment to nearby marine mammals and sea turtles. The report data received from the companies will be used to increase the knowledge base on species habitat.

For all seismic operations in water depths >200 m in the Western Planning Area (WPA) and CPA, and all water-depths in the Eastern Planning Area (EPA), this NTL requires the use of soft start or ramp-up and visual observers as required in the previous NTL's. This NTL includes requirements for

(1) seismic vessels to have at least two visual observers on watch during all daylight hours when geophysical operations are being conducted;

(2) visual observers to have completed a training course;

(3) no additional duties to be assigned to visual observers during their watch;

(4) limiting watch and duty hours for observers;

(5) elements that must be included in the training course;

(6) methods to be employed for visual observations;

(7) "all clear" prior to ramp-up;

(8) shutdown of seismic airguns when whales are within 500 m of the center of the airgun array;

(9) restart of survey after shutdown; and

(10) reporting required information, including types of reports and submission of reports to MMS.

This NTL also contains special provisions for borehole, or vertical seismic profiling, operations and a special mitigation exception for seismic vessels that employ experimental passive acoustic monitoring.

Biologically Sensitive Areas of the Gulf of Mexico (NTL 2004-G05)

The Live Bottom (Pinnacle Trend) Stipulation and Topographic Features Stipulation are now embodied in the more comprehensive NTL 2004-G05, Biologically Sensitive Areas of the Gulf of Mexico. In addition to existing stipulated areas for biological features, a new category of protected area has been established under NTL 2004-G05 termed "Potentially Sensitive Biological Features." These are hard-bottom features not protected by a biological lease stipulation that are of moderate to high relief (about 8 ft or higher), provide surface area for the growth of sessile invertebrates, and can attract large numbers of fish. These features would be located outside any "No Activity Zone" of any of the named topographic features (banks) or the 70 live-bottom (pinnacle trend) stipulated blocks.

Structure-Removal Operations (NTL 2004-G06)

The Structure-Removal Operations NTL (NTL 2004-G06) provides lessees with updated information on Endangered Species Act (ESA) consultations and the monitoring and reporting requirements to be followed by the operators and severance subcontractors during decommissioning operations. This NTL also addresses MMS's position on decommissionings using explosive-severance tools in light of the recent expiration of Marine Mammal Protection Act (MMPA) take-regulations (50 CFR 216.141-147).

As detailed in the NTL, MMS currently permits decommissioning operations conditional on two Biological Opinions (BO) from NOAA Fisheries subsequent to consultations conducted under Section 7 of the ESA. Issued in July 1988, the "generic" consultation BO and its Incidental Take Statement (ITS) identifies the terms and conditions of operation for explosive-severing activities using charges that range from >5 to 50 lb (http://www.gomr.mms.gov/homepg/regulate/environ/generic-consultation.pdf). In October 2003, NOAA Fisheries issued a second BO, the "de minimus" BO, that lists minimization measures that apply to explosive-severing charges ≤0-5 lb (http://www.gomr.mms.gov/homepg/regulate/environ/de-minimus-consultation.pdf). Both BO's define specific operational criteria that explosive-severing activities must follow. These criteria include

(1) the use of high-velocity explosives (i.e., detonation rates >7,600 m per second);

(2) a maximum of eight individual blasts per group of detonations;

(3) blast staggering at an interval of 0.9 seconds (900 milliseconds);

(4) charge placement no less than 15 ft below the mudline (BML); and

(5) maximum charge sizes of either 5 lb (for the "de minimus" consultation) or 50 lb (for the "generic" consultation).

This NTL contains special provisions to lessees applying for permits on decommissioning operations suggesting activities that do not fall within the above-listed criteria. Discussion is also made on the specific penalties prescribed under the ESA and MMPA when an unauthorized take (i.e., harassment, harm, injury, or mortality) of a marine mammal or sea turtle occurs. Ultimately, the conditions described under and referenced within this NTL aid in reducing the chance of harassment or injury to marine mammals and sea turtles in the vicinity of removal activities.

Deepwater Ocean Current Monitoring on Floating Facilities (Proposed NTL)

Recently a limited number of high-speed, ocean water current events, at times approaching 2 kt, were observed at depths exceeding 1,500 m in the northern GOM (Hamilton et al., 2003; USDOI, MMS 2002 and 2003). Similar high-speed current events have been identified in ongoing MMS current measurement studies in the north-central GOM. In addition, high-speed current events do not appear to be an isolated or exceptionally unusual occurrence in the northern GOM. Mega-furrows on the seafloor have been discovered in the northern GOM, apparently because of the erosional effects of high-speed currents. Further, several deepwater oil and gas operators also have observed very high-speed midwater jets exceeding 150 cm per second over the upper continental slope. Causes of these jet events remain uncertain until further data is collected (Dimarco et al., 2004).

Ocean current speeds used by industry in the design, operation, and function of mobile offshore drilling units (MODU's), floating production platforms, and their ancillary equipment (i.e., drilling and production risers, tendons, and mooring systems) may have been underestimated in the past. At some locations in the GOM, 10-year Loop Current events have been exceeded and, in certain instances, deep ocean currents were not measured or underestimated current speeds were considered in designs. Recent incidents have demonstrated to the MMS GOM Region a need for more site-specific data for use in hindcasting and forecasting ocean currents that may affect structural design, fatigue criteria, or daily operations.

The MMS has drafted a new NTL (Deepwater Ocean Current Monitoring on Floating Facilities) relevant to these concerns; it is expected to be issued October 2004 and effective April 2005. The new NTL establishes and implements the following program to monitor ocean currents and share the data for all floating MODU's and production facilities operating or installed in waters depths >400 m (1,312 ft).

Floating MODU's

(1) Floating MODU's will continuously monitor and gather ocean current data on a real-time basis from near the ocean surface (~30 m (100 ft)) to ~1,000 m (3,280 ft) using an Acoustic Doppler Current Profile (ADCP) current monitoring system or comparable equipment, mounted as near to the ocean surface as practicable.

(2) During drilling operations, if currents are measured with speeds >0.75 kt at the maximum range of the ADCP (or comparable equipment) for more than 24 hours, all current data below the maximum range of the ADCP will be monitored and gathered while any remotely operated vehicle (ROV) operations or inspections are conducted. An ADCP or point current meter installed on the ROV will be used to obtain data on all ROV operations or inspections until the well is completed.

(3) In water depths >1,100 m (3,608 ft), a current meter, preferably an upward looking ADCP, must be installed near the ocean bottom (~100 m (328 ft) from the seafloor). Data collected by floating MODU's must be recorded and reported to an industry-accessible Internet website.

Planned Floating Production Facilities

Prior to installing a planned floating production facility, a full water-column mooring must be deployed to collect at least one year of site-specific current data at the planned floating production facility location. These current data must extend from near the ocean surface (~30 m (100 ft)) to near the ocean bottom (~100 m (328 ft) from the seafloor). The moorings should include point current meters spaced no more than 500 m (1,640 ft) apart, an ADCP array, or some combination of point current meters and ADCP's. Data should be time averaged as specified in the NTL, which also describes what must be reported to an industry-accessible Internet website. Data collected during the drilling phase may be used as part of the one year of site-specific current data.

Existing Floating Production Facilities

(1) An ADCP current monitoring system or comparable equipment must be used to continuously monitor and gather ocean current data on a real-time basis from near the surface (~30 m (100 ft)) to ~1,000 m (3,280 ft) for existing floating production facilities. The ADCP (or comparable equipment) must be mounted as near to the ocean surface as possible. Details of time averaging, data processing, and reporting to an industry-accessible Internet website are discussed in the NTL.

(2) Floating production facilities located in water depths >1,100 m (3,608 ft) must install a current meter, preferably an upward looking ADCP, to continuously monitor and record speed and direction of the near-bottom current (~100 m (328 ft) from the seafloor). Once every 6 months and whenever a near-bottom current event >1 kt is presumed to have occurred, the data must be retrieved and examined. Whenever average currents >1 kt are measured for more than 24 hours by any component, the MMS GOM Region Technical Assessment and Operation Support (TAOS) Section must be immediately notified and a full water-column mooring must be installed that contains point current meters spaced no more than 500 m (1,640 ft) apart, an ADCP array, or some combination of point current meters and ADCP's. Details of time averaging, data processing, and reporting to an industry-accessible Internet website are discussed in the NTL.

(3) Operators of existing floating production facilities must provide to the MMS GOM Region TAOS Section by January 1, 2005, the monitoring equipment type, the date of installation, the depth range of the monitoring equipment, and the Internet website address where the operator proposes to publish the data.

Suggested methods for data time averaging and the reporting of any current data that is not required are specified in the NTL. The NTL also lists exclusions from the above requirements and other details related to data collection and reporting.

4.   IMPACT ANALYSIS

4.1. UPDATE OF PROJECTIONS OF POTENTIAL ACTIVITY FROM THE PROPOSED ACTION

4.1.1. Resource Estimates and Timetables

The multisale EIS discusses projections for activities associated with a typical proposed CPA lease sale. The estimated amounts of resources projected to be leased, discovered, developed, and produced as a result of the proposed CPA Lease Sale 194 are 0.276-0.654 BBO and 1.590-3.300 Tcf of natural gas. The oil and gas resource projections and associated activities used in the multisale EIS are based on the *2000 Assessment of Conventionally Recoverable Hydrocarbon Resources of the Gulf of Mexico and Atlantic Outer Continental Shelf as of January 1, 1999* (Lore et al., 2001). The MMS is currently in the process of updating the 2000 National Resource Assessment and has recently revised the deep gas resource estimate on the shelf. This revision is based on knowledge gained from recent deep drilling activity in this area, prompting the addition of a new "Deep Shelf Mesozoic" play to the assessment. Although MMS anticipates a significant increase in total undiscovered conventionally recoverable deep gas resources on the shelf as reported, a significant portion of these newly assessed deep gas resources are either currently under lease or are uneconomic at this time. The MMS GOM Region's Office of Resource Evaluation reviewed the oil and natural gas resource projections and associated activities for CPA Lease Sale 194 and confirmed that they are still valid; they are therefore incorporated by reference.

4.1.2. Hurricane Lili

As discussed in **Chapter 1.5.** of the multisale EIS, criteria, models, and procedures for shutdown operations and the orderly evacuation of personnel prior to a pending hurricane have been in place on the GOM OCS for more than 30 years. Operating experience from extensive drilling activities and the presence of more than 4,000 platforms during the 30-plus years of the GOM OCS Program has proven the effectiveness and safety of securing wells and evacuating a facility in advance of severe weather conditions. This was evident in early October 2002 when Hurricane Lili, a Category 4 hurricane, passed near 800 OCS structures in the GOM. Of 800 structures, 6 were seriously damaged. All six were more than 20 years old. Of the 99 drilling rigs in the GOM at that time, 4 sustained substantial damage. About 25,000 offshore workers were safely evacuated (USDOI, MMS, 2002c).

Nine pollution events occurred as a result of Hurricane Lili. The only significant incident was a 350-barrel (bbl) oil spill at Ship Shoal Block 119. The other eight pollution events ranged from 0.14 gal to 3 bbl. In August 2003, MMS published a report that recorded the transport and fate of oil spilled at Ship Shoal Block 119 during Hurricane Lili (USDOI, MMS, 2003a). The report states that the lessee mounted an appropriate response and the response was complicated by hurricane-related onshore conditions. Approximately 145 bbl of oil were recovered and 205 bbl of oil dissipated. No shoreline or wildlife impacts were reported. No birds were fouled. The unrecovered oil was removed from the surface of the water by natural weathering processes including evaporation, dissolution in the water, adsorption to particulate material, and biodegradation. The lessee, Murphy Exploration and Production Company, the U.S. Coast Guard, the Louisiana Oil Spill Coordinator's Office, oil-spill-response organizations, and MMS have discussed the response (Bedell, 2004).

4.1.3. Louisiana's Artificial Reef Program

Louisiana passed legislation in 2002 requiring that the Louisiana Artificial Reef Program be reviewed and recommendations be made to improve and revise the program where necessary. Public hearings were held in March and April 2003 for offshore shrimpers to identify areas where artificial reefs would not interfere with shrimping. The 2003 public hearings, held across the state by the Louisiana Department of Wildlife and Fisheries (LDWF), were reported to be poorly attended.

In response to the State legislation, the LDWF reconvened a Louisiana Artificial Reef Initiative (LARI) committee to review, discuss, and provide recommendations to the Louisiana Artificial Reef Council in an effort to update the LDWF Artificial Reef Program. Four recommendations to the Council were made by the LARI committee:

(1) establish deepwater (>400 ft) artificial reef sites;

(2) reconfigure the existing nine artificial reef planning areas;

(3) establish a committee to evaluate the Special Artificial Reef Sites (SARS) — Amendment 2; and

(4) establish an inshore (shore to 100 ft) artificial reef working group.

The Artificial Reef Council approved deepwater reef sites and an inshore reef working group. The Council deferred the LARI committee's recommendation to reconfigure the existing reef planning areas to create smaller planning areas, which would target areas of higher density of platforms. No action was taken by the Council on the LARI committee's recommendation to establish a committee comprised of representatives of the shrimping industry, oil and gas industry, MMS, biologists, and various other user groups for evaluation of the permitting of SARS.

4.1.4. Geological and Geophysical Activities

Geological and geophysical activities are performed to obtain information on surface and near-surface geology and on subsurface geologic formations. The MMS has completed a programmatic EA (PEA) on G&G activities in the GOM (USDOI, MMS, 2004a). The activities analyzed in the PEA include seismic surveys, deep-tow side-scan surveys, electromagnetic surveys, geological and geochemical sampling, and remote-sensing surveys. The impact-producing factors considered in the PEA include seismic survey noise, vessel and aircraft noise, seafloor disturbance, and space-use conflicts with seismic arrays. The notice of availability of the PEA was published in the *Federal Register* on July 30, 2004. The results of the analyses in the PEA are that G&G activities are not expected to result in significant adverse impacts to any of the potentially affected resources. The EA resulted in a Finding of No Significant Impact.

4.1.5. Structure Removal Operations

The MMS is preparing a PEA to assess the potential impacts that decommissioning activities, related to the severing and removal of seafloor obstructions and facilities (i.e., wellheads, caissons, casing strings, platforms, mooring devices, etc.) and subsequent salvage operations, have on the GOM. Preparation of the PEA is an important step in the decision process for future permitting for the removal of offshore structures and for further consultation and coordination with other Federal agencies. The PEA will be used as part of the rulemaking process by NOAA for incidental take regulations under Subpart I of the MMPA and to initiate consultation for explosive severance activities under Section 7 of the ESA. Topics of primary concern to be addressed in the PEA include pre-severance operations, severance technologies, industry needs related to water depth and location, and the potential impacts of decommissioning operations on the marine environment. On April 16, 2003, MMS published a Notice of Preparation in the *Federal Register* requesting information or issues that should be addressed in the PEA. Several comments were received with most centering on the need for increased "rigs-to-reef" options and concerns over NEPA procedure. The PEA is scheduled for completion in the Fall of 2004.

4.2. UPDATE OF INFORMATION ON THE AFFECTED ENVIRONMENT

Chapter 3 and Appendix 9 of the multisale EIS provide a complete description as of 2002 of the affected environment for the proposed lease sale and are incorporated by reference (USDOI, MMS, 2002b). For a number of resources (geology, meteorology, air quality, water quality, coastal barrier beaches and associated dunes, wetlands, deepwater benthic communities, topographic features, sea turtles, coastal and marine birds, fish resources, public services, infrastructure, land-use plans, sociocultural issues and environmental justice, commercial fisheries, recreational resources and beach use, archaeological resources, and coastal zone management plans), MMS has identified no new information since completion of the multisale EIS.

The following summarizes the affected environment for resources MMS has determined should be reevaluated because of new information that was unavailable during the preparation of the multisale EIS. This includes information on protective measures for protected species, estimated population numbers of cetaceans in the GOM, designation of critical habitat for the Gulf sturgeon, a revised oil-spill probability for the snowy plover, proposed liquefied natural gas (LNG) projects, and proposed sand dredging projects.

4.2.1. Marine Mammals

Chapter 3.2.4. of the multisale EIS discusses nonendangered/nonthreatened and endangered/ threatened species of marine mammals known to occur in the GOM. Five mysticete (or baleen) whales (the northern right, blue, fin, sei, and humpback), one odontocete (or toothed) whale (the sperm whale), and one sirenian (the West Indian manatee) are listed as endangered. Sperm whales are common in the oceanic waters of the northern GOM. Sightings in all seasons and recent tag results indicate that there may be a resident population in the GOM in addition to migratory visitors. Baleen whales are not common. All five of the endangered baleen whales that occur in the GOM are considered rare or extralimital (Würsig et al., 2000). The most frequently observed baleen whale in the GOM is the nonendangered Bryde's whale; it is considered uncommon in GOM waters. The West Indian manatee *(Trichechus manatus)* inhabits only coastal marine, brackish, and freshwater areas.

For over a decade, MMS has funded and participated in research on marine mammals in the GOM. This research has included the GulfCet I and GulfCet II studies conducted in 1992-1999, the Sperm Whale Acoustic Monitoring Program (SWAMP) in 2000-2001, and the ongoing Sperm Whale Seismic Survey (SWSS) study initiated in 2002. Through these studies, the diverse cetacean community of the

GOM has been documented, including the year-round sperm whale population. Many of these cruises included tissue sampling of numerous GOM cetacean species for genetic analysis.

New information from NOAA Fisheries concerning estimated population numbers for cetaceans in the northern GOM is presented in **Table 1** (USDOC, NOAA Fisheries, 2004). This is the first update by NOAA Fisheries in several years and more specific than the relative occurrence estimates provided in the multisale EIS.

Since the new estimates are in agreement with the relative occurrence estimates presented in the multisale EIS, no new analysis is required as a result of the new estimates. **Chapter 4.3.2.1.** of this EA reevaluates the proposed action's potential impact on marine mammals with the Protected Species Stipulation and NTL's described in **Chapter 3.3**.

Table 1
Estimated Abundance of Cetaceans in the Northern GOM Oceanic Waters

Species	Common Name	Estimated Number of Individuals
Balaenoptera edeni	Bryde's whale	42
Physeter macrocephalus	Sperm whale	1,315
Kogia spp.	Dwarf or pygmy sperm whale	809
Ziphius cavirostris	Cuvier's beaked whale	88
Unidentified ziphiid	Unidentified beaked whales	98
Feresa attenuata	Pygmy killer whale	443
Pseudorca crassidens	False killer whale	1,515
Orcinus orca	Killer whale	180
Globicephala sp.	Pilot whale	3,252
Peponocephala electra	Melonheaded whale	3,320
Grampus griseus	Risso's dolphin	1,777
Tursiops truncatus	Bottlenose dolphin	26,852
Steno bredanensis	Rough-toothed dolphin	2,469
Lagenodelphis hosei	Fraser's dolphin	698
Stenella frontalis	Atlantic spotted dolphin	39,545
Stenella longirostris	Spinner dolphin	11,550
Stenella attenuate	Pantropical spotted dolphin	93,174
Stenella clymene	Clymene dolphin	16,439
Stenella coeruleoalba	Striped dolphin	6,258

Source: USDOC, NOAA Fisheries, 2004.

4.2.2.   Sea Turtles

Five species of sea turtles are known to inhabit the waters of the GOM: the green, the loggerhead, the hawksbill, the Kemp's ridley, and the leatherback (Pritchard, 1997). All sea turtle species inhabiting the GOM are listed as either endangered or threatened under the ESA of 1973 (Pritchard, 1997). **Chapter 3.2.5.** of the multisale EIS presents information on the distribution, habitat, feeding, and nesting of sea turtles. **Chapter 4.4.2.2.** of this EA reevaluates the proposed action's potential impact on sea turtles with the Protected Species Stipulation and NTL's described in **Chapter 3.3**.

4.2.3.   Gulf Sturgeon Critical Habitat Designation

In 1991, the Gulf sturgeon (*Acipenser oxyrinchus desotoi*) was listed as threatened. A recovery plan was developed to ensure the preservation and protection of Gulf sturgeon spawning habitat (USDOI, FWS, and Gulf States Marine Fisheries Commission, 1995). On April 18, 2003, critical habitat for the Gulf sturgeon was designated in Louisiana, Mississippi, Alabama, and Florida. The designation was published in the *Federal Register* on March 19, 2003. Critical habitat identifies specific areas that are essential to the conservation of Gulf sturgeon and that may require special management considerations or protections. Fourteen geographic areas among the GOM rivers and tributaries were designated critical habitat. These areas encompass approximately 2,783 river km (1,730 river mi) and 6,042 km² (2,333 mi²) of estuarine and marine habitat. The estuarine and marine critical habitat units extend from Lake Borgne in Louisiana to Suwannee Sound in Florida. Major shipping channels have been excluded in the Lake Borgne and Pensacola Bay critical habitat units. Gulf sturgeon are discussed in **Chapter 3.2.8.** of the multisale EIS. **Chapter 4.4.2.3.** of this EA evaluates the proposed action's potential impact on Gulf sturgeon critical habitat and reevaluates the potential impact with the Protected Species Stipulation and NTL's described in **Chapter 3.3**.

4.2.4. Snowy Plover

Coastal and marine birds are discussed in **Chapter 3.2.7.** of the multisale EIS. The snowy plover inhabits the areas identified in **Figure 3**. When commenting on the Draft EIS for EPA Lease Sales 189 and 197, published after the multisale EIS, FWS stated that snowy plover are present year round (USDOI, MMS, 2003b) as opposed to the period (February to August) that was used for the multisale EIS and the EPA Draft EIS. **Chapter 4.4.2.4.** of this EA reevaluates the proposed action's potential impact on snowy plover given this new information.

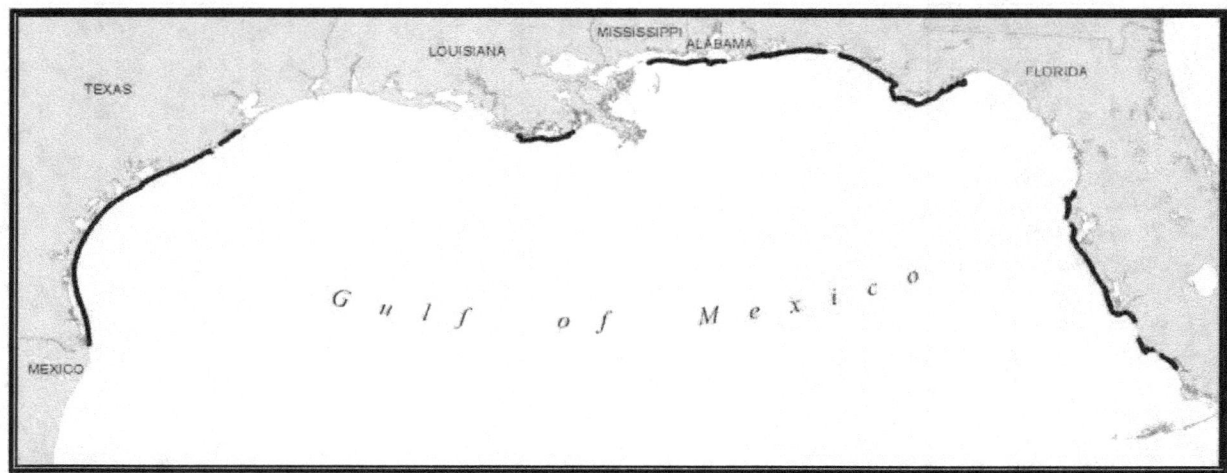

Figure 2.   Snowy Plover Habitat.

4.3.   UPDATE OF POTENTIAL CUMULATIVE ACTIVITIES

4.3.1.   Liquefied Natural Gas Projects

Chapter 4.1.1.3.8.6., Alternative Transportation Methods of Natural Gas, of the multisale EIS discusses LNG. In late 2002, the Deepwater Ports Act (DWPA) was modified to include the establishment of natural gas ports on the OCS (the Maritime Transportation Security Act of 2002, Public Law 107-295, November 2002). The DWPA requires an applicant to file a deepwater port license application with the Secretary of the U.S. Department of Transportation (USDOT). The USDOT Secretary has delegated the authority to process an application to the U.S. Coast Guard (USCG) and to the Maritime Administration (MARAD). To date, these agencies have received six applications for LNG ports in the GOM. All of the proposed receiving terminals are located within the CPA. **Table 2** provides a brief description of each of the proposed projects.

Specific information about each application can be obtained from the USDOT Internet website (http://www.dms.dot.gov) by using the USDOT Docket Number provided in **Table 2** or by using the project name in a "simple search." All of the proposed LNG receiving terminals, except the Energy Bridge, plan to use a gravity-based structure (GBS) to store LNG and to support regasification equipment. The Energy Bridge Project proposes to use a floating system.

Table 2
LNG Applications in the GOM

Project Name	Affiliations	Preferred Location (Area and Block)	Projected Start-Up Date	USDOT Docket Number
Port Pelican	ChevronTexaco	Vermilion 140	2Q 2006	14134
Energy Bridge	Excelerate Energy	West Cameron 603	1Q 2005	14294
Gulf Landing	Shell US Gas & Power	West Cameron 213	Jan 2009	16860
Compass Port	ConocoPhillips	Mobile Pass 910	Early 2009	17659
Main Pass Energy Hub	Freeport McMoRan Energy	Main Pass 299	Dec 2007	17696
Pearl Crossing	ExxonMobil	West Cameron 220	4Q 2008	18474

4.3.2. Sand Dredging Projects

The MMS has evaluated the use of sand resources from Ship Shoal Blocks 87, 88, 89, 94, and 95, and South Pelto Blocks 12, 13, 14, 18, and 19 for levee and barrier island restoration projects. As a result, MMS may enter into noncompetitive, negotiated sand and gravel leases with a third party on these blocks. In CPA Lease Sale 190, held in March 2004, MMS leased Ship Shoal Blocks 87, 88, and 89 with a stipulation to mitigate possible conflicts between sand dredging and oil and gas activities. The stipulation requires lessees to notify MMS in writing and to consult with the Chief, MMS Leasing Division, prior to construction or placement of any structure for exploration and development in areas leased for sand dredging. These activities include, but are not limited to, anchoring, well drilling, and pipeline and platform emplacement.

The MMS will determine whether the planned activities conflict with ongoing or planned sand dredging operations. If MMS determines that a lessee's planned activities conflict with sand dredging, MMS will require the lessee to conduct its operations in a manner to avoid such conflicts. The MMS will coordinate the activities of dredge and service vessels in order to minimize conflicts. The other blocks listed above (Ship Shoal Blocks 94 and 95 and South Pelto Blocks 12, 13, 14, 18, and 19) are also currently under lease. Should they become available for oil and gas leasing in the future, MMS would consider adoption of this stipulation for those blocks.

Ship Shoal Multi-Project EA

On July 6, 2004, MMS announced in the *Federal Register* the availability of an EA examining three separate sand dredging projects in the CPA (USDOI, MMS, 2004b). The EA resulted in a finding of no significant impact (FONSI). The proposed actions are to dredge approximately 15.5 million yd^3 of OCS sand from Ship Shoal, an ancient and submerged barrier island. Two potential borrow areas are located approximately 10 mi (16 km) south of Isle Dernieres and the central coast of Louisiana (**Figure 3**). Each borrow polygon is approximately 10 mi^2.

Two of the proposed leases are intended for the Louisiana Department of Natural Resources or Terrebonne Parish, Louisiana, for up to 3.5 million yd^3 of sand for the beach nourishment projects at New Cut and Whiskey Island in the Isles Dernieres barrier arc (**Figure 3**). These restoration projects are expected to benefit a maximum total of 1,341 ac (543 ha) of beach and adjacent tidal marsh and wetlands. The expected commencement dates for these projects are Spring of 2005.

One proposed lease is intended for the U.S. Army Corps of Engineers (COE) for 12 million yd^3 of sand for the Morganza levee project. This project is scheduled to begin late in 2004 and involves sand removal during 20 months of continuous dredging and temporary storage inland at two impoundment sites in Terrebonne Parish near Houma, Louisiana. Levee construction would proceed over 12 years.

Mitigations for the multiple Ship Shoal projects are discussed in **Chapter 4.8.6.** below.

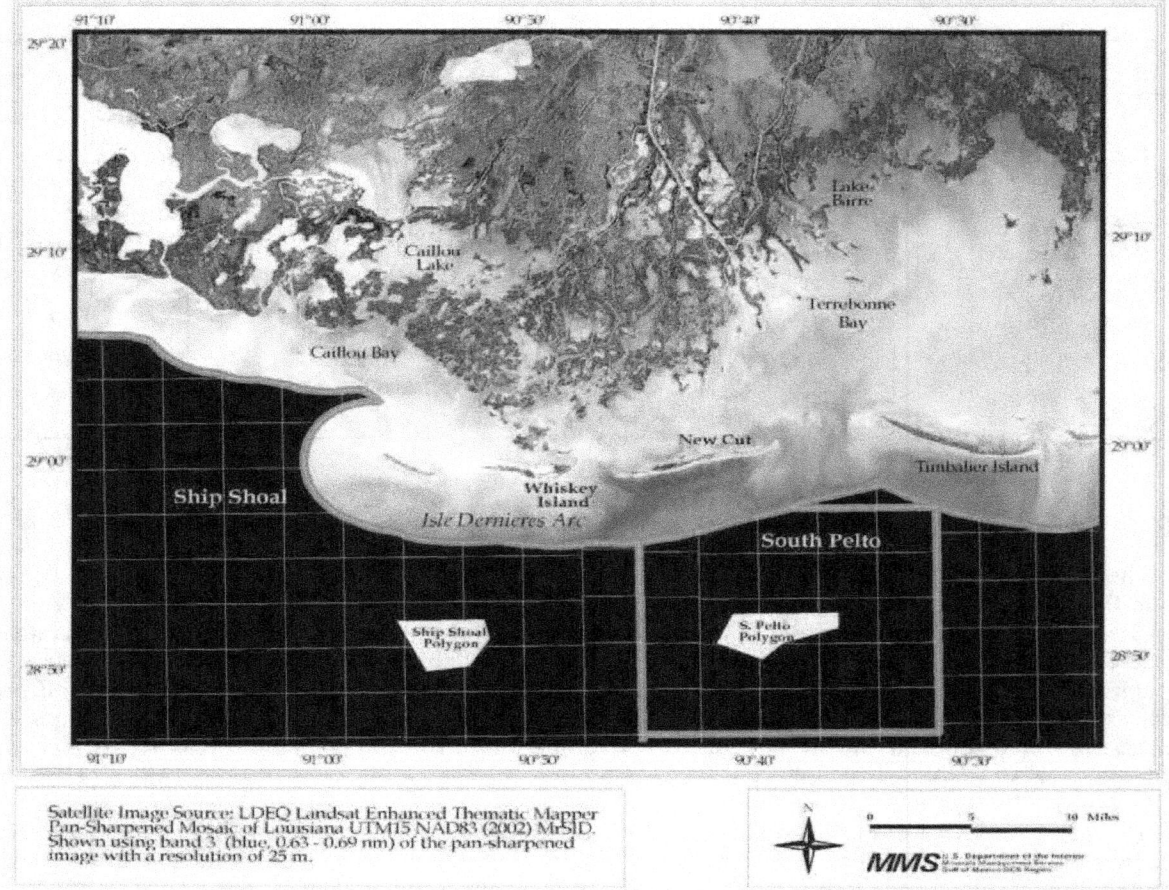

Figure 3.   Satellite Image of Coastal Louisiana Shoreline Showing (1) the Location of the Isles Dernieres
           Barrier Island Arc, (2) the Whiskey Island/New Cut Tidal Channel Locations for Beach
           Restoration Projects, and (3) the Proposed OCS Sand Borrow Polygons.

Pelican Island and Pass La Mer to Chaland Pass EA

The MMS participated as a cooperating agency in the preparation of an EA by NOAA Fisheries for a barrier island restoration project in western Plaquemines Parish, Louisiana (USDOC, NMFS, 2003). The project (Pelican Island and Pass La Mer to Chaland Pass) proposes to use approximately 2.6 million yd^3 of sand for beach nourishment and wetland reconstruction as part of the Barataria Barrier Island Complex Project under the 1990 Coastal Wetlands Planning, Protection, and Restoration Act (CWPPRA). It is expected to benefit a total of 868 ac (351 ha). Sand borrow locations would be located in West Delta Blocks 25 and 49. The MMS anticipates entering into noncompetitive, negotiated leases with the State of Louisiana to use OCS sand resources for this CWPPRA project. The project was scheduled to begin in Spring 2004; because of the ongoing mitigation discussions between MMS and NOAA Fisheries, a delay of 6-12 months is expected.

4.4.   IMPACTS FROM ALTERNATIVE A—THE PROPOSED ACTION

4.4.1.   Summary of Analysis Incorporated by Reference from the Multisale EIS

The multisale EIS analyzed the effects of a typical CPA lease sale by presenting a set of ranges for resource estimates, projected exploration and development activities, and impact-producing factors for any of the proposed CPA lease sales held over the 5-year period. This EA tiers off the multisale EIS and incorporates that document by reference. All unleased blocks in the CPA will be available for lease under the proposed action (as described in **Chapter 3.1.**). The MMS expects only a small percentage of blocks would be leased, and an even smaller percentage would actually produce oil and gas. The following is a summary of impacts to resources taken from the multisale EIS.

4.4.1.1. Impacts on Coastal Resources

No significant impacts to the physical shape and structure of barrier beaches and associated dunes are expected to occur as a result of the proposed action. Should a spill contact a barrier beach, sand removal during cleanup activities is expected to be minimal.

Adverse initial impacts and more importantly secondary impacts of pipeline and navigation canals are considered the most significant proposed-action-related impacts to wetlands. Although initial impacts are considered locally significant and are largely limited to where OCS-related canals and channels pass through wetlands, secondary impacts may have substantial, progressive, and cumulative adverse impacts to the hydrologic basin or subbasin in which they are found. Offshore oil spills resulting from the proposed action are not expected to significantly damage inland wetlands. The greatest threat to wetland habitat is from an inland spill from a vessel accident or pipeline rupture. While a resulting slick may cause minor impacts to wetland habitat, equipment and personnel used to clean up a slick over the impacted area may generate the greatest direct impacts to the area.

Normal OCS activities are expected to have little adverse impact on seagrass communities. Impacts from pipeline installation activities are expected to be very small and short-term. Inshore spills from vessel collisions or pipeline ruptures pose the greatest potential threat to seagrass communities.

No significant impacts to listed beach mice are expected to occur as a result of the proposed action. Adverse impacts to Alabama, Choctawhatchee, St. Andrew, and Perdido Key beach mice are unlikely. Impacts may result from consumption of beach trash and debris. No direct impacts from oil spills are expected. Protective measures required under the ESA should prevent any oil-spill-response and cleanup activities from having significant impact to the beach mice and their habitat.

Adverse impacts on endangered/threatened and nonendangered/nonthreatened coastal and marine birds are expected to be sublethal. These effects include behavior changes, eating OCS-related contaminants or discarded debris, and displacement of localized groups from optimal habitats. Chronic sublethal stress, however, is often undetectable in birds. As a result of stress, individuals may weaken and be prone to infection or disease, have reduced reproductive success, or have disturbed migration patterns. Oil spills pose the greatest potential direct and indirect impacts to coastal and marine birds. If physical oiling of individuals or local groups of birds occurs, some degree of both acute and chronic physiological stress associated with direct and secondary uptake of oil would be expected. Low levels of oil could stress birds by interfering with food detection, feeding impulses, predator avoidance, territory definition, homing of migratory species, susceptibility to physiological disorders, disease resistance, growth rates, reproduction, and respiration. Reproductive success can be affected by the toxins in oil. Indirect effects occur by fouling of nesting habitat, and displacement of individuals, breeding pairs, or populations to less favorable habitats. Dispersants used in spill cleanup activity can have toxic effects similar to oil on the reproductive success of coastal and marine birds. The air, vehicle, and foot traffic that takes place during shoreline cleanup activity can disturb nesting populations and degrade or destroy habitat.

Routine activities resulting from the proposed action are expected to have little impact on Gulf sturgeon. Impacts on Gulf sturgeon may occur from resuspended sediments and OCS-related discharges. Contact with spilled oil could cause irritation of gill epithelium and production of metabolites toxic to the liver in Gulf sturgeon.

Impacts to coastal water quality from the proposed action are expected to be minimal. The primary impacting sources to water quality in coastal waters are point-source and nonpoint-source discharges from OCS support facilities and support-vessel discharges.

Emissions of pollutants into the atmosphere from the activities associated with the proposed action are not projected to have significant impacts on onshore air quality. Emissions from OCS activity are not expected to have concentrations that would change onshore air-quality classifications. Increases in onshore annual average concentrations of NO_x, SO_x, and PM_{10} are estimated to be less than the maximum increases allowed in the PSD Class I or II areas.

The impact from the proposed action on Gulf Coast recreational beaches is expected to be minimal. The proposed action may result in an incremental increase in noise from helicopter and vessel traffic, nearshore operations that may adversely affect the enjoyment of some Gulf Coast beach uses, and some increases in beached debris; these impacts are expected to have little effect on the number of beach users. Impacts from oil spills are expected to be short-term and localized; a large volume of oil contacting a recreational beach could close the area to recreational use for up to 30 days.

Routine activities associated with the proposed action are not expected to impact coastal historic archaeological resources. It is very unlikely that an oil spill would occur and contact coastal historic archaeological sites from accidental events associated with the proposed action. The major effect from an oil spill impact would be visual contamination of a historic coastal site, such as a historic fort or lighthouse. As historic archaeological sites are protected under law, it is expected that any spill cleanup operations would be conducted in such a way as to cause little or no impacts to historic archaeological resources. These impacts would be temporary and reversible.

The proposed action is not expected to result in impacts to coastal prehistoric archaeological sites; however, should such an impact occur, unique or significant archaeological information could be lost. It is very unlikely that an oil spill would occur and contact coastal, barrier island prehistoric sites as a result of the proposed action. Should a spill contact a prehistoric archaeological site, unique or significant archaeological information could be irreversibly damaged or lost; damage might include loss of radiocarbon-dating potential, direct impact from oil-spill cleanup equipment, and/or looting. Previously unrecorded sites could be impacted by oil-spill cleanup operations on beaches.

Some economic indicators in the GOM Region have changed since the multisale EIS. Both oil and natural gas prices have increased substantially, with natural gas prices more than doubling. As of July 21, 2004, Henry Hub Natural Gas closed at $5.895 per million British thermal unit (Btu) and West Texas Intermediate at $40.83 per barrel (Oilnergy, 2004). While activity in the ultra-deep waters of the GOM (>5,000 ft) has remained fairly strong, the number of rigs operating in the region and the number of wells drilled have continued a downward trend. Since 2002, the average number of rigs operating in water depths of 1,000-4,999 ft has declined by 29 percent and the number of wells drilled is down by 37 percent. Offshore service vessel utilization and day rates have also declined, with supply boats experiencing the most dramatic change. Supply boat average day rates in May 2004 ranged from $3,875 for boats <200 ft and $5,010 for boats ≥ 200 ft, with utilization rates of 70 and 73 percent, respectively (Greenberg, 2004). In contrast, the July 2001 rates ranged from $7,718 for boats <200 ft and $10,950 for boats ≥ 200 ft, with utilization rates of 89 and 100 percent, respectively.

Activities resulting from the proposed action are expected to minimally affect the analysis area's land use, infrastructure, or demographic characteristics of the Gulf coastal communities. The proposed action is expected to generate less than a 1 percent increase in employment in the Texas, Louisiana, Mississippi, and Alabama subareas. Nowhere would these impacts be significant because demand will be met primarily with the existing population and available labor force. Accidental events such as oil or chemical spills, blowouts, and vessel collisions would have no effects on land use or demographics. Coastal or nearshore spills could have short-term adverse effects on coastal infrastructure requiring cleanup of any oil or chemicals spilled. The opportunity costs associated with oil-spill cleanup activities are expected to be temporary and of short duration.

Five different classes of relevant OCS activities exist in the region: transportation corridors, oil and natural gas pipelines, petroleum bulk storage facilities, shipyards, and a natural gas processing plant. A large portion of OCS-related infrastructure is located in south Lafourche Parish where the Houma Indian population is clustered (Hemmerling et al., 2003; USDOI MMS; 2003). Proposed CPA Lease Sale 194 would not significantly alter this pre-existing situation where onshore cumulative effects already exist. Therefore, since the preexisting situation would not be significantly altered, minority and low-income populations would not sustain disproportionate adverse effects from the proposed action.

4.4.1.2. Impacts on Offshore Environments

Adverse impacts to pinnacles or topographic features from routine activities resulting from the proposed action are not expected because the Live Bottom (Pinnacle Trend) and Topographic Features Stipulations establish requirements for setbacks from these features. Adverse impacts from accidental seafloor oil releases or blowouts are expected to be rare because drilling and pipeline operations are not permitted in the vicinity of pinnacles or topographic features and because both pinnacles and topographic features are small in size and dispersed within the areas that they occur; no community-wide impacts are expected. If contact were to occur between diluted oil and adult sessile biota, including coral colonies in the case of the Flower Garden Banks, the effects would be primarily sublethal and there would be limited incidents of mortality.

No adverse impacts to the ecological function or biological productivity of the widespread, low-density chemosynthetic communities or to the widespread, typical, deep-sea benthic communities are expected to occur as a result of routine activities or accidental events resulting from the proposed action. The potential for adverse impacts to the rarer, widely scattered, high-density, Bush Hill-type chemosynthetic communities are expected to be greatly reduced by the requirement for OCS activities to avoid potential chemosynthetic communities by a minimum of 1,500 ft (NTL 2000-G20). High-density chemosynthetic communities could experience minor impacts from drilling discharges or resuspended sediments located at more than 1,500 ft away.

Impacts to marine water quality occur from discharges of drilling fluids and cuttings during exploration and produced water during production. Impacts to marine water quality are expected to be minimal as long as all regulatory requirements are met. Spills <1,000 bbl are not expected to significantly impact marine water quality. Larger spills, however, could impact marine water quality. Chemical spills, the accidental release of synthetic-based drilling fluids (SBF), and blowouts are expected to have temporary localized impacts on marine water quality. The U.S. Environmental Protection Agency (USEPA) National Pollution Discharge Elimination System (NPDES) general permit for the CPA expired November 3, 2003, and is in the process of being reissued. The draft general permit was published July 7, 2004; a 3-year permit rather than a 5-year permit has been proposed. A study will be conducted during the 3-year permit term to learn more about the potential impacts of increased produced-water discharge to the hypoxic zone in the future. The final permit issuance is expected before the end of 2004.

The NPDES general permit has been administratively continued until reissuance of the new permit so that operators with existing permit coverage remained covered. Operators without existing permit coverage can eliminate discharges by barging waste to shore, reinjecting the waste, or seeking coverage in one of three ways. Operators can apply directly to USEPA for an individual permit. Operators can obtain coverage through a Transfer Agreement in which an operator with permit coverage transfers coverage to the noncovered operator. Lastly, operators who discharge without a NPDES permit, but meet the terms and conditions of the expired permit, can apply for an Administrative Compliance Order. Under this case, the operator has committed a minor paperwork violation and would possibly incur penalties of $2,000/month.

Emissions of pollutants into the atmosphere from offshore facilities are not expected to impact significantly offshore air quality because of emission heights and rates. Accidents involving high concentrations of H_2S could result in deaths as well as environmental damage. Other emissions of pollutants into the atmosphere from accidental events as a result of the proposed action are not projected to have significant impacts.

The routine activities related to the proposed action are not expected to have long-term adverse effects on the size and productivity of any marine mammal species or population stock endemic to the northern GOM. Routine OCS activities are expected to have impacts that are sublethal. A small number of marine mammals could be harmed or killed by chance collisions with service vessels or by eating indigestible trash and debris from proposed-action-related activities. Lethal "takes" as a result of explosive removal of OCS platform or production facilities are not expected because of established mitigation measures. While no adverse impacts of seismic operations have been documented in the GOM, MMS and NOAA Fisheries have established mitigation measures as a precaution to reduce the potential for injury to protected species. Populations of marine mammals in the northern Gulf are expected to be exposed to residuals of oils spilled as a result of the proposed action during their lifetimes. Chronic or acute exposure may result in the harassment, harm, or mortality to marine mammals occurring in the northern Gulf. In most foreseeable cases, exposure to hydrocarbons persisting in the sea following the dispersal of an oil slick will result in sublethal impacts to marine mammals.

The routine activities resulting from the proposed action are unlikely to have significant adverse effects on the size and recovery of any sea turtle species or population in the GOM. Routine activities are expected to have sublethal impacts. Adverse impacts are localized degradation of water quality from operational discharges near platforms; noise from helicopters, service vessels, platform, and drillship operations; and hatchling disorientation caused by brightly-lit platforms. Sea turtles could be harmed or killed from chance collisions with service vessels and from eating floating debris from proposed-action-related activities. Lethal "takes" because of explosive removals of OCS facilities are expected to be rare because of established mitigation measures (e.g., NOAA Fisheries Observer Program). Accidental blowouts, oil spills, and spill-response activities resulting from the proposed action have the potential to impact small to large numbers of sea turtles in the GOM. Populations of sea turtles in the northern Gulf will be exposed to residuals of oils spilled as a result of the proposed action during their lifetimes. Chronic or acute exposure may result in the harassment, harm, or mortality to sea turtles occurring in the northern Gulf. In most foreseeable cases, exposure to hydrocarbons persisting in the sea following the dispersal of an oil slick will result in sublethal impacts to sea turtles. Death would likely occur to sea turtle hatchlings exposed to, becoming fouled by, or consuming tarballs.

A less than 1-percent decrease in fish resources and/or standing stocks or in essential fish habitat (EFH) would be expected as a result of the proposed action. Coastal and marine environmental degradation resulting from the proposed action is expected to have little effect on fish resources or EFH. Recovery of fish resources and EFH can occur from more than 99 percent, but not all, of the expected coastal and marine environmental degradation. Fish populations, if left undisturbed, would regenerate in one generation, but any loss of wetlands as EFH would be permanent. Impacts are expected to result in less than a 1-percent change in commercial fishing "pounds landed" or in the value of landings. Oil spills estimated to result for the proposed action would cause less than a 1-percent decrease in standing stocks of any population, commercial fishing efforts, landings, or value of those landings. The resultant impact on fish populations and commercial fishing activities within the CPA would be negligible and indistinguishable from variations due to natural causes. Any affected commercial fishing activity would recover within 6 months.

Routine activities associated with the proposed action are not expected to impact offshore historic or prehistoric archaeological resources. The greatest potential impact to an offshore historic archaeological resource would result from direct contact between an offshore activity and a historic shipwreck. Offshore oil and gas activities resulting from the proposed action could contact a shipwreck because of incomplete knowledge on the location of shipwrecks in the Gulf. Although this occurrence is not probable, such an event could result in the disturbance or destruction of important historic archaeological information. Should an offshore prehistoric archaeological site be contacted by proposed-action-related activities, unique or significant archaeological information could be lost.

4.4.2. Updated Impact Analysis for the Proposed Action

The following chapters describe the potential impacts as a result of the proposed action for those resources (marine mammals, sea turtles, Gulf sturgeon, and snowy plover) where new information became available after MMS prepared the multisale EIS. The analyses for these resources have been reevaluated taking into consideration the new information.

4.4.2.1. Marine Mammals

The Protected Species Stipulation and the three related NTL's (Chapters 3.3.1-3.3.2.) were not analyzed in the multisale EIS because they were not in place at the time the EIS was completed. The purpose of the Protected Species Stipulation is to reduce the potential taking of federally protected species, while the three NTL's serve to provide detailed guidance relative to the requirements of the Protected Species Stipulation. These mitigation measures are precautionary and intended to further reduce the potential for any impacts related to the proposed action to occur. The environmental impacts of the proposed action on marine mammals given the Protected Species Stipulation and NTL's remain the same as presented in the multisale EIS.

The multisale EIS stated that small numbers of marine mammals could potentially be killed or injured by chance collision with service vessels and by eating indigestible debris, particularly plastic items, lost from service vessels, drilling rigs, and fixed and floating platforms. Deaths as a result of structure removals are not expected because of existing mitigation measures or those being developed for structures placed in oceanic waters. There is no conclusive evidence whether anthropogenic noise has or has not caused long-term displacements of, or reductions in, marine mammal populations. Contaminants in waste discharges and drilling muds might indirectly affect marine mammals through food-chain biomagnification, although the scope of effects and their magnitude are not known. The routine activities of the proposed action are not expected to have long-term adverse effects on the size and productivity of any marine mammal species or population stock endemic to the northern GOM.

Accidental blowouts, oil spills, and spill-response activities resulting from the proposed action have the potential to impact marine mammals in the GOM. Characteristics of impacts (i.e., acute vs. chronic impacts) depend on the magnitude, frequency, location, and date of accidents; characteristics of spilled oil; spill-response capabilities and timing; and various meteorological and hydrological factors. Populations of marine mammals in the northern GOM will be exposed to residuals of oils spilled as a result of the proposed action during their lifetimes. Chronic or acute exposure may result in the harassment, harm, or mortality to marine mammals occurring in the northern GOM. In most foreseeable cases, exposure to hydrocarbons persisting in the sea following the dispersal of an oil slick will result in sublethal impacts (e.g., decreased health, reproductive fitness, and longevity; and increased vulnerability to disease) to marine mammals.

4.4.2.2. Sea Turtles

The Protected Species Stipulation and the three related NTL's (**Chapters 3.3.1-3.3.2.**) were not analyzed in the multisale EIS because they were not in place at the time the EIS was completed. The purpose of the Protected Species Stipulation is to reduce the potential taking of federally protected species, while the three NTL's serve to provide detailed guidance relative to the requirements of the Protected Species Stipulation. These mitigation measures are precautionary and intended to further reduce the potential for any impacts related to the proposed action to occur. The environmental impacts of the proposed action on sea turtles given the Protected Species Stipulation and NTL's remain the same as presented in the multisale EIS.

The multisale EIS stated that routine activities resulting from the proposed action have the potential to harm individual sea turtles. These animals could be impacted by the degradation of water quality resulting from operational discharges; noise generated by helicopter and vessel traffic, platforms, and drillships; brightly-lit platforms; explosive removals of offshore structures; vessel collisions; and jetsam and flotsam generated by service vessels and OCS facilities. Lethal effects are most likely to be from chance collisions with OCS service vessels and ingestion of plastic materials. "Takes" as a result of explosive removals are expected to be rare because of mitigation measures already established (e.g., NOAA Fisheries Observer Program) and in development. Most OCS activities are expected to have sublethal effects. Contaminants in waste discharges and drilling muds might indirectly affect sea turtles through food-chain biomagnification, although there is uncertainty concerning the possible effects. Chronic sublethal effects (e.g., stress) resulting in persistent physiological or behavioral changes and/or avoidance of impacted areas could cause declines in survival or fecundity, and population; however, such declines are not expected. The routine activities of the proposed action are unlikely to have significant adverse effects on the size and recovery of any sea turtle species or population in the GOM.

4.4.2.3. Gulf Sturgeon Critical Habitat Designation

The Protected Species Stipulation and the three related NTL's (**Chapters 3.3.1-3.3.2.**) were not analyzed in the multisale EIS because they were not in place at the time the EIS was completed. The purpose of the Protected Species Stipulation is to reduce the potential taking of federally protected species, while the three NTL's serve to provide detailed guidance relative to the requirements of the Protected Species Stipulation. These mitigation measures are precautionary and intended to further reduce the potential for any impacts related to the proposed action to occur. The environmental impacts of the proposed action on Gulf sturgeon and critical habitat given the Protected Species Stipulation and NTL's remain the same as presented in the multisale EIS.

The multisale EIS stated that Gulf sturgeon critical habitat in the GOM has been designated in Louisiana, Mississippi, Alabama, and Florida. The estuarine and marine critical habitat units extend from Lake Borgne in Louisiana to Suwannee Sound in Florida. The coastal area analyzed in the multisale EIS comprises the known locations of Gulf sturgeon (**Figure 5**). This area is slightly larger and encompasses the Gulf sturgeon critical habitat. The probability of an oil spill ≥1,000 bbl occurring and contacting known locations of the Gulf sturgeon within 10 days as a result of the proposed action is 2-5 percent. Contact with spilled oil could cause irritation of gill epithelium and production of metabolites toxic to the liver in Gulf sturgeon. Other potential impacts on Gulf sturgeon and critical habitat may occur from resuspended sediments (channel dredging and coastal pipeline installation) and OCS-related discharges, as well from nonpoint runoff from estuarine OCS-related facilities. Should a spill occur and contact the Gulf sturgeon habitat, it is expected to minimally impact the Gulf sturgeon because of the low toxicity of this pollution and almost absent overlap between individual Gulf sturgeon and occurrence of contamination. Routine activities resulting from the proposed action are expected to have little potential effect on Gulf sturgeon and critical habitat.

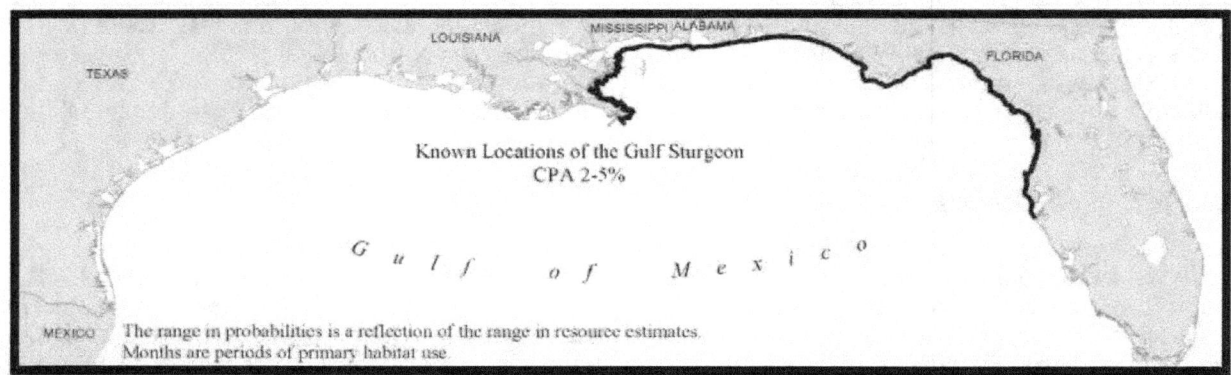

Figure 4.   Probability of Oil Spills (≥1,000 bbl) Occurring and Contacting within 10 Days Known Locations of Gulf Sturgeon as a Result of the Proposed Action.

4.4.2.4. *Snowy Plover*

According to FWS, the snowy plover is present at its identified habitats year round as opposed to only February through August. Therefore, the oil-spill probability for the snowy plover was recalculated for this EA. The recalculated probability of an oil spill ≥1,000 bbl occurring and contacting snowy plover habitat within 10 days as a result of the proposed action is 2-5 percent. While this is an increase from the February through August probability (2-4%) as shown on **Figure 4-21** of the multisale EIS, the environmental impacts of the proposed action remain the same as presented in the multisale EIS.

The multisale EIS stated that oil spills from the proposed action pose the greatest potential direct and indirect impacts to snowy plover. Birds that are heavily oiled usually die. If physical oiling of individuals or local groups of birds occurs, some degree of both acute and chronic physiological stress associated with direct and secondary uptake of oil would be expected. Small coastal spills, pipeline spills, and spills from accidents in navigated waterways can contact and affect the snowy plover. Lightly oiled birds can sustain tissue and organ damage from oil ingested during feeding and grooming or from oil that is inhaled. Stress and shock enhance the effects of exposure and poisoning. Low levels of oil could stress snowy plover by interfering with food detection, feeding impulses, predator avoidance, territory definition, susceptibility to physiological disorders, disease resistance, growth rates, reproduction, and respiration. Reproductive success can be affected by the toxins in oil. Indirect effects occur by fouling of nesting habitat, and displacement of individuals, breeding pairs, or populations to less favorable habitats. Dispersants used in spill cleanup activity can have toxic effects similar to oil on the reproductive success of snowy plover. The air, vehicle, and foot traffic that takes place during shoreline cleanup activity can disturb nesting populations and degrade or destroy habitat.

4.5.   ALTERNATIVE B—THE PROPOSED ACTION EXCLUDING THE BLOCKS NEAR BIOLOGICALLY SENSITIVE TOPOGRAPHIC FEATURES

Alternative B would offer for lease all unleased blocks in the CPA, as described for the proposed action, with the exception of any unleased blocks within the 167 blocks in the CPA that are subject to the Topographic Features Stipulation. All the assumptions including the potential mitigating measures and resource estimates remain the same as in the proposed action. The environmental impacts of this alternative remain the same as presented in the multisale EIS (**Chapter 4.2.2.**).

4.6. ALTERNATIVE C—THE PROPOSED ACTION EXCLUDING THE UNLEASED BLOCKS WITHIN 15 MILES OF THE BALDWIN COUNTY, ALABAMA, COAST

Alternative C would offer for lease all unleased blocks in the CPA, as described for the proposed action, with the exception of any unleased blocks within 15 mi of the coast of Baldwin County, Alabama. Although the blocks to be excluded contain oil and/or natural gas resources, this alternative would not change the resource estimate and activity ranges for the overall proposed actions. The environmental impacts of this alternative remain the same as presented in the multisale EIS (**Chapter 4.2.3.**).

4.7. ALTERNATIVE D—NO ACTION

Alternative D is equivalent to cancellation of the proposed lease sale. The opportunity for development of the estimated of 0.276-0.654 BBO and 1.590-3.300 Tcf of natural gas that could have resulted from the proposed action would be precluded or postponed, and any potential environmental impacts resulting from the proposed action would not occur or would be postponed.

Canceling the proposed lease sale would eliminate the effects described for Alternative A (the proposed action). However, other sources of energy would substitute for the lost production. Principal substitutes would be additional imports, conservation, additional domestic production, and switching to other fuels. These alternatives, except conservation, would have substantial negative environmental impacts of their own. These substitutes and the effects are discussed in the multisale EIS and *Energy Alternatives and the Environment* (USDOI, MMS, 2001), and are incorporated by reference. The environmental impacts of this alternative remain the same as presented in the multisale EIS (**Chapter 4.2.4.**).

4.8. CUMULATIVE ANALYSIS

The cumulative analysis considers the effects of impact-producing factors related to the proposed action, prior and future OCS sales, State oil and gas activities, other governmental and private projects and activities, and pertinent natural processes and events that may occur and adversely affect environmental and socioeconomic resources. Descriptions of these activities and the analysis of the cumulative effects are included in the multisale EIS.

4.8.1. Marine Mammals

The cumulative conclusions for marine mammals remain unchanged from the multisale EIS. Activities considered under the cumulative scenario could affect protected cetaceans and sirenians. These marine mammals could be impacted by the degradation of water quality resulting from operational discharges; vessel traffic; noise generated by platforms, drillships, helicopters, and vessels; seismic surveys; explosive structure removals; oil spills; oil-spill-response activities; loss of debris from service vessels and OCS structures; commercial fishing; capture and removal; and pathogens. The cumulative impact on marine mammals is expected to result in a number of chronic and sporadic sublethal effects (behavioral effects and nonfatal exposure to or intake of OCS-related contaminants or discarded debris) that may stress and/or weaken individuals of a local group or population and predispose them to infection from natural or anthropogenic sources. Few deaths are expected from oil spills, chance collisions with OCS service vessels, ingestion of plastic material, commercial fishing, and pathogens. Oil spills of any size are estimated to be recurring events that would periodically contact marine mammals. Deaths as a result of structure removals are not expected to occur because of mitigation measures (e.g., NOAA Fisheries Observer Program). Disturbance (noise from vessel traffic and drilling operations, etc.) and/or exposure to sublethal levels of toxins and anthropogenic contaminants may stress animals, weaken their immune systems, and make them more vulnerable to parasites and diseases that normally would not be fatal. The net result of any disturbance would be dependent upon the size and percentage of the population likely to be affected, ecological importance of the disturbed area, environmental and biological parameters that influence an animal's sensitivity to disturbance and stress, or the accommodation time in response to prolonged disturbance (Geraci and St. Aubin, 1980). Collisions between cetaceans and ships, though expected to be rare events, could cause serious injury or mortality.

The incremental contribution of impacts stemming from the proposed action is expected to be primarily sublethal (behavioral effects and nonfatal exposure to or intake of OCS-related contaminants or discarded debris). Effects of the incremental contribution of the proposed action combined with non-OCS activities may be deleterious, as stated in the multisale EIS, to cetaceans occurring in the GOM. Biological significance of any mortality would depend, in part, on the size and reproductive rates of the affected stocks, as well as the number, age, and size of animals affected.

4.8.2. Sea Turtles

The cumulative conclusions for sea turtles remain unchanged from the multisale EIS. Activities considered under the cumulative scenario may harm sea turtles and their habitats. Those activities include structure installation, dredging, water quality and habitat degradation, OCS-related trash and flotsam, vessel traffic, seismic surveys, explosive structure removals, oil spills, oil-spill-response activities, natural catastrophes, pollution, dredge operations, vessel collisions, commercial and recreational fishing, human consumption, beach lighting, and power plant entrainment. Sea turtles could be killed or injured by chance collision with service vessels or eating marine debris, particularly plastic items, lost from OCS structures and service vessels. It is expected that deaths as a result of structure removals would rarely occur because of mitigation measures (e.g., NOAA Fisheries Observer Program). The presence of, and noise produced by, service vessels and by the construction, operation, and removal of drill rigs may cause physiological stress and make animals more susceptible to disease or predation, as well as disrupt normal activities. Contaminants in waste discharges and drilling muds might indirectly affect sea turtles through food-chain biomagnification, although there is uncertainty concerning the possible effect. Oil spills and oil-spill-response activities are potential threats that may be expected to cause turtle deaths. Contact with, and consumption of, oil and oil-contaminated prey may seriously impact turtles. Sea turtles have been seriously harmed by oil spills in the past. The majority of OCS activities are estimated to be sublethal (behavioral effects and nonfatal exposure to intake of OCS-related contaminants or debris). Chronic sublethal effects (e.g., stress) resulting in persistent physiological or behavioral changes and/or avoidance of impacted areas could cause declines in survival or productivity, resulting in either acute or gradual population declines. The incremental contribution of the proposed action to cumulative impacts on sea turtles is slight.

4.8.3. Gulf Sturgeon Critical Habitat Designation

The Gulf sturgeon cumulative analysis includes analysis of the critical habitat, which was designated after the multisale EIS was published. However, since Gulf sturgeon critical habitat is within the area analyzed by the multisale EIS, the Gulf sturgeon conclusion, including the impact contribution by the proposed action, has not changed (**Chapters 4.2.1.9.** and **4.4.3.9.** of the multisale EIS). The Gulf sturgeon can be impacted by activities considered under the cumulative scenario such as oil spills, alteration and destruction of habitat, and commercial fishing. The effects from contact with spilled oil will be sublethal and last for less than one month. Substantial damage to Gulf sturgeon critical habitat is expected from inshore alteration activities and natural catastrophes. The FWS (50 CFR 17) identified the following activities that may destroy or adversely modify Gulf sturgeon critical habitat:

(1) Actions that would appreciably reduce the abundance of riverine prey for larval and juvenile sturgeon, or of estuarine and marine prey for juvenile and adult Gulf sturgeon, within a designated critical habitat unit. Such actions include dredging, dredged material disposal, channelization, in-stream mining, and land uses that cause excessive turbidity or sedimentation.

(2) Actions that would appreciably reduce the suitability of Gulf sturgeon spawning sites for egg deposition and development within a designated critical habitat unit. Such actions include impoundment, hard-bottom removal for navigation channel deepening, dredged material disposal, in-stream mining, and land uses that cause excessive sedimentation.

(3) Actions that would appreciably reduce the suitability of Gulf sturgeon riverine aggregation areas, also referred to as resting, holding, and staging areas, used by

adult, subadult, and/or juveniles, believed necessary for minimizing energy expenditures and possibly for osmoregulatory functions. Such actions include dredged material disposal upstream or directly within such areas and other land uses that cause excessive sedimentation.

(4) Actions that would alter the flow regime (the magnitude, frequency, duration, seasonality, and rate-of-change fresh water discharge over time) of riverine critical habitat unit such that appreciably impaired for the purposes Gulf sturgeon migration, resting, staging, breeding site selection, courtship, egg fertilization, egg deposition, and egg development. Such actions include impoundment, water diversion, and dam operations.

(5) Actions that would alter water quality within a designated critical habitat unit, including temperature, salinity, pH, hardness, turbidity, oxygen content, and other chemical characteristics, such that it is appreciably impaired for normal Gulf sturgeon behavior, reproduction, growth, or viability. Such actions include dredging; dredged material disposal; channelization; impoundment; in-stream mining; water diversion; dam operations; land uses that cause excessive turbidity; and release of chemicals, biological pollutants, or heated effluents into surface water or connected groundwater via point sources or dispersed nonpoint sources.

(6) Actions that would alter sediment quality within a designated critical habitat unit such that it is appreciably impaired for normal Gulf sturgeon behavior, reproduction, growth, or viability. Such actions include dredged material disposal, channelization, impoundment, in-stream mining, land uses that cause excessive sedimentation, and release of chemical or biological pollutants that accumulate in sediments.

(7) Actions that would obstruct migratory pathways within and between adjacent riverine, estuarine, and marine critical habitat units. Such actions include dam construction, dredging, point-source-pollutant discharges, and other physical or chemical alterations of channels and passes that restrict Gulf sturgeon movement.

If any of the above were to occur and result in damage to Gulf sturgeon critical habitat, it is expected that the Gulf sturgeon will experience a decline in population sizes and a displacement from their current distribution that will last more than one generation. Deaths of adult sturgeon are expected to occur from commercial fishing. The incremental contribution of the proposed action to the cumulative impact is negligible because the effect of contact between sale-specific oil spills and Gulf sturgeon is expected to be sublethal and last less than one month.

4.8.4. Snowy Plover

The cumulative conclusions for the snowy plover remain unchanged from the multisale EIS. It is expected that cumulative effects would be detrimental to the snowy plover; however, the majority of effects from the major impact-producing factors on the snowy plover are sublethal (behavioral effects and nonfatal exposure to or intake of OCS-related contaminants or discarded debris) and would usually cause temporary disturbances and displacement of localized groups inshore. The net effect of habitat loss from oil spills, new construction, and maintenance and use of pipeline corridors and navigation waterways would reduce the overall carrying capacity of disturbed area(s) in general. The incremental contribution of the proposed action to the cumulative impact is negligible because the effects of the most probable impacts, such as lease sale-related operational discharges and helicopters and service-vessel noise and traffic, are estimated to be sublethal with some displacement of local individuals or groups. It is expected that there would be little interaction between OCS-related oil spills and the snowy plover. The cumulative effect on snowy plover is expected to result in declines in the numbers of birds that form localized groups.

4.8.5. Liquefied Natural Gas Projects

An EIS was prepared (or is currently being prepared) for all but one of the proposed LNG terminals located in the GOM; an EA was prepared for the Energy Bridge project. All of the proposals with a GBS component have similar impact-producing factors and potential effects on GOM resources. The Energy Bridge floating system decreases the possibility of adverse effects to the benthic communities. The following information examines the common factors of the proposals and briefly describes a combination of adverse and beneficial effects of varying duration that may occur as a result of licensing a proposed project.

Long-term, minor adverse impacts on air quality would be expected; emissions though would not exceed annual USEPA-permitted emissions levels and not adversely affect the air quality of onshore nonattainment areas. Short- and long-term minor adverse effects from noise would be expected. However, any such effects are expected to be minimal and temporary. A combination of long-term and short-term, minor adverse impacts on water quality would be expected. Discharge from vessels and onshore facilities would be the primary sources of effects on water quality in coastal waters.

Short- and long-term, minor adverse effects on biological resources would be expected; none of the expected impacts though would be significant. Long-term, minor adverse and minor beneficial impacts on recreational resources would be expected. These LNG projects, however, are not expected to displace recreational fishing in the vicinity of the deepwater ports. No impacts on shore-related recreational activities would be anticipated. Effects would also occur with respect to commercial fisheries.

No effects on archaeological resources would be expected. Geotechnical surveys have been conducted on the preferred locations for the proposed terminal areas and pipeline routes. Local short-term minor and long-term negligible adverse effects to geological resources would be expected. Deepwater port applicants have tried to choose terminal locations where the potential for hydrocarbon accumulations were considered to be low.

Short- and long-term, minor adverse effects and short-term, minor beneficial effects would be expected on socioeconomic conditions. The proposals would not cause adverse environmental impacts or disproportionate human health effects on minority and/or low-income communities.

Long-term, minor adverse impacts on transportation would be expected because of increased vessel and helicopter traffic. No effects would be expected in connection with reliability and safety issues. Applicants use hazard identification and management techniques to minimize the potential for unanticipated events.

4.8.6. Sand Dredging Projects

Multiple sand dredging projects using approximately 15.5 million yd^3 of OCS sand have been proposed for Ship Shoal (USDOI, MMS, 2004b). Ship Shoal has an estimated 216 mi^2 of crest area with sand thickness >1 m. Estimates of the amount of sea bottom disturbed to remove the sand ranges from <900 ac (1.4 mi^2) to >6,400 ac (10 mi^2) for the three projects. Neither the sand volume nor the estimated area disturbed are significant. Modeling indicates that very large volumes of sand could be removed from Ship Shoal with no adverse effects on sensitive coastal resources.

The potential impacts from the proposed New Cut/Whiskey Island beach nourishment and Morganza levee projects focus on (1) sea turtles, (2) disturbance to prehistoric and historical archaeological resources that may be present in the shallow waters of Ship Shoal, and (3) space-use conflicts on the OCS because of 25 mi of existing oil and gas pipelines that cross or border the designated sand borrow polygons. All other physical, biological, and socioeconomic resources are expected to experience minimal to no impacts from these proposed projects.

As discussed in the EA, potential impacts would be addressed by the following mitigation measures:

(1) requiring stipulations to protect sea turtles when it is determined that there is a likelihood of sea turtle presence within the area during the dredging operation and a trailing suction hopper dredge is used;

(2) avoiding potential historic archaeological site locations identified in both the Ship Shoal and South Pelto areas through a remote-sensing survey conducted previously;

(3) sampling and monitoring dredge material from borrow sites to identify and protect possible prehistoric resources;

(4) establishing a minimum "no dredge" setback distance of 1,000 ft (305 m) from existing pipelines; and

(5) requiring the use of an electronic positioning system on the dredge vessels and transmittal of location and production information to MMS.

The potential impacts from the proposed Pelican Island and Pass La Mer to Chaland Pass dredging and the beach restoration project are expected to be similar to those for the Ship Shoal dredging projects. General mitigations were identified in the EA (USDOC, NMFS, 2003; Table 13), but specific quantitative setbacks from OCS infrastructure, such as pipelines and platforms, are expected to be part of the negotiated lease agreement and a FONSI announcement. The MMS has undertaken studies to examine the appropriateness of various setback distances that can be used for dredging operations in proximity to OCS infrastructure. The 1,000-ft (305-m) setback to be used for the Ship Shoal projects is a conservative limitation made in the absence of a specific examination of the issue.

5. CONSULTATION AND COORDINATION

5.1. SCOPING FOR THE ENVIRONMENTAL ASSESSMENT FOR THE CENTRAL PLANNING AREA'S PROPOSED LEASE SALE 194

The MMS performs ongoing external and internal scoping in order to determine the breadth and depth necessary for environmental analysis.

External Scoping: The scoping process for this EA was formally initiated on June 4, 2004, with the *Federal Register* notice announcing the preparation of an EA. In the notice, MMS requested that interested parties submit comments regarding any new information or issues that should be addressed in the EA. The comment period closed on July 6, 2004. No responses were received. Scoping and coordination efforts, though, continue throughout the lease sale process and have been conducted since the publication of the multisale EIS:

- On January 8 and 9, 2003, public hearings were held on the Draft EIS for EPA Lease Sales 189 and 197 (USDOI, MMS, 2003b) in New Orleans, Louisiana, and Mobile, Alabama.

- The MMS held the GOM Region's annual Information Transfer Meeting in January 14-16, 2003. Sessions pertained to MMS's GOM OCS oil and gas program, as well as regional environmental, social, and economic concerns, and current OCS industry activities and technologies.

- The MMS co-hosted the International Offshore Pipeline Workshop on February 26-28, 2003, which brought together worldwide experience in operating and regulating offshore oil and gas activities in order to identify/disseminate pipeline issues and knowledge for continued safe and pollution free operations.

- On June 1-3, 2003, MMS participated in the Oceanology International Americas conference in New Orleans, Louisiana. The conference incorporated the following disciplines: marine science, technology, operational oceanography, policy, and education.

- On June 4, 2003, MMS published a Notice of Preparation of an EA on proposed CPA Lease Sale 190. In the notice, MMS requested interested parties to submit comments regarding any new information or issues that should be addressed in the EA. No comments were received.

- In June 2003, MMS requested the Gulf States' review MMS's GOM Region Studies Development Plan for FY 2004-2006. On July 16, 2003, comments were received from the Louisiana Department of Natural Resources.

- To ensure conformance with State Coastal Zone Management (CZM) program policies and local land-use plans, MMS prepares appropriate consistency documents for each proposed OCS lease sale. On October 28, 2003, MMS sent the Consistency Determination (CD) for CPA Lease Sale 190 to the Governors of Louisiana, Mississippi, and Alabama, and to the head of each State's CZM group. The States confirmed MMS's Consistency Statement for CPA Lease Sale 190. On September 4, 2003, MMS met with Louisiana's CZM group; September 9, 2003, with Mississippi; and September 10, 2003, with Alabama.

- In October 2003, MMS published the EA for CPA Lease Sale 190 (USDOI, MMS, 2003c). No comments were received of the EA.

- On November 18-20, 2003, MMS participated in the Thirteenth Annual Clean Gulf Conference along with consultants, responders, and Federal and State agencies. The MMS made the following presentations: "The Oil Spill Response Equipment," "Oil Spill Exercises and Drills," "Updates of the MMS Worst Case Discharge for Blowouts and Pipelines," and "Ongoing Exploration Along the US/Mexican International Boundary."

- On November 19, 2003, MMS published a Notice of Preparation of an EA on proposed WPA Lease Sale 192. In the notice, MMS requested interested parties to submit comments regarding any new information or issues that should be addressed in the EA. No comments were received.

- A workshop on social and economic topics related to the oil and gas industry was hosted by the MMS GOM Region on February 3-5, 2004, in New Orleans, Louisiana. Discussions were structured around the following topics: Industry Trends and Dynamics; Community-Level Impacts of Oil and Gas in the Gulf of Mexico Region; and Cultural Impacts of Oil and Gas Activity in the Gulf of Mexico. Information derived from the workshop will be used to shape future research projects. The proceedings will be published on the MMS Internet website in the near future.

- In March 2004, MMS published the EA for WPA Lease Sale 192 (USDOI, MMS, 2004c). No comments were received on the EA.

- On March 3, 2004, the Louisiana Sand Management Working Group, composed of Federal, State, and local authorities, academia, and industry, met to provide advice to MMS relative to the long-term use of Federal sand offshore Louisiana. Louisiana's coastal landloss problem continues at a rate of more than 25-30 mi^2 per year, severely affecting the storm buffering capacity and the protection that nearshore barrier islands provide to human populations, oil and gas infrastructure, inland bays, estuaries, and wetlands. A major concern expressed by Louisiana is the potential conflict created by emplacement of oil and gas infrastructure in areas of rich sand deposits. The MMS is currently evaluating the issue. The MMS evaluates each proposal for space-use conflicts, recommends mitigations for affected resources and to alleviate conflicts with existing OCS infrastructure such as pipelines and platforms. **Chapter 4.1.3.2.2.** of the multisale EIS discusses MMS's Sand Resources Programs.

- On July 9, 2004, the COE released a Draft Programmatic EIS (PEIS) for the Louisiana Coastal Area (LCA) Ecosystem Restoration Plan with a 45-day comment period. The LCA Plan is designed to be a coordinated approach to alleviate and arrest the chronic and severe loss of wetlands along coastal Louisiana. The draft PEIS envisions a range of "restoration opportunities" over the next 10 years that fall into two categories: those that divert Mississippi River water and sediment to naturally replenish threatened areas and habitats, and those that reconstruct or enhance geomorphic barriers that dampen storm waves and tidal surge, such as barrier islands and levee systems. The COE's preferred alternative, or Tentatively Selected Plan, is an ambitious synergistic combination of projects undertaking both river diversions and geomorphic restorations estimated to cost $1.9 billion over 10 years. The MMS is commenting on the draft PEIS, focusing primarily on conflicts and interfaces with MMS's OCS Program.

- On June 4, 2004, MMS published a Notice of Preparation of an EA on proposed EPA Lease Sale 197. In the notice, MMS requested interested parties to submit comments regarding any new information or issues that should be addressed in the EA. No comments were received.

- On July 26, 2004, MMS met with the Florida Department of Environmental Protection in Tallahassee, Florida, to discuss the EA for EPA Lease Sale 197 and tiering the CD for the EPA Lease Sale 197 CD to the previous EPA Lease Sale 189 CD.

Internal Scoping: Internal scoping is an ongoing activity for all environmental projects and NEPA documents. Part of internal scoping involves reviewing resource estimates and oil-spill modeling results used in the preparation of the multisale EIS to determine if they are still valid. The MMS GOM Region's Office of Resource Evaluation reviewed the oil and gas resource projections and associated activities for CPA Lease Sale 194 and confirmed that they remain within the range of those projected by MMS for a "typical CPA lease sale." The MMS Headquarters' Oil-Spill Risk Analysis (OSRA) group confirmed that results from the OSRA model summarized in the multisale EIS and presented in a separate MMS report (USDOI, MMS, 2002d) are still valid for the proposed lease sale.

Internal scoping also requires MMS subject matter experts/analysts and NEPA coordinators to continuously update their knowledge base and incorporate three primary informational components into their analyses:

(1) recent studies/reports;

(2) monitoring results; and

(3) related cumulative-impact data.

The MMS's analysts and coordinators take an active role in the preparation, execution, and peer review of studies and reports developed under MMS's Environmental Studies Program. In addition, some analysts provide expertise and are involved in additional studies and analyses conducted by other Federal/State agencies and universities concerning GOM issues and interests. The information obtained from these studies, as well as other relevant, non-MMS research, was considered by each subject matter expert in their assessment for this EA. **Appendix C** of the multisale EIS lists the GOM Region studies published from 1999-2002, while **Appendix B** of this EA lists those GOM studies published since the completion of the multisale EIS. Technical summaries for these studies are available on the MMS Internet website (http://www.gomr.mms.gov/homepg/regulate/environ/techsumm/rec_pubs.html).

In addition to hindcasting projections and estimates, MMS compliance monitoring tracks the status of mitigation and other conditions applied to approved-OCS activities. The monitoring information received from field inspections, office auditing, and/or mandatory reporting is reviewed by MMS analysts. Knowledge gained through environmental compliance monitoring forms a basis for mitigation revision and future mitigation development, and was ultimately incorporated by analysts into this EA.

Cumulative analyses are prepared by MMS subject matter experts that consider activities that could occur and may adversely affect GOM resources, including proposed CPA Lease Sale 194, prior and future OCS lease sales, State oil and gas activities, and other governmental and private projects and activities. The MMS analysts are often responsible for reviewing GOM activities not associated with oil and gas operations. All information gained from cumulative analyses was considered by MMS analysts in their assessments for this EA.

5.2. CONSULTATION AND COORDINATION CALENDAR

A complete description of all consultation and coordination activities and meetings is included in Chapter 5 of the multisale EIS. A brief summary of these events follows:

Multisale EIS Process

September 12, 2001

The Call for Information/Notice of Intent (Call/NOI) for the proposed 2003-2007 CPA and WPA lease sales was published in the *Federal Register*. The required 30-day comment period closed on October 12, 2001. Additional public notices were distributed via newspaper notices, mailed notices, and the Internet. The MMS received four comment letters in response to the Call. Ten written scoping letters were received in response to the NOI.

October 25-22, 2001

The MMS held scoping meetings in Galveston and Houston, Texas; New Orleans, Louisiana; and Mobile, Alabama, to receive comments on the Draft EIS for the proposed 2003-2007 CPA and WPA lease sales. A summary of comments presented at the scoping meetings is provided in **Chapter 5.3.** of the multisale EIS.

April 15, 2002 and
April 17, 2002

The MMS, by memorandum to FWS (April 15, 2002) and NOAA Fisheries (April 17, 2002), requested formal Section 7 consultation for CPA Lease Sales 185, 190, 194, 198, and 201, and WPA Lease Sales 187, 192, 196, and 200. The consultation included all aspects of oil and gas exploration, development, production, and abandonment activities. The FWS concluded that the proposed actions are not likely to jeopardize the continued existence of listed species under FWS jurisdiction (whooping crane, Gulf sturgeon, brown pelican, Alabama beach mouse, Perdido Key beach mouse, loggerhead sea turtle, piping plover, and Kemp's ridley sea turtle) and are not likely to destroy or adversely modify their designated critical habitat, if any. For each species with designated critical habitat, the adverse effects that may occur to critical habitat would be temporary in nature and of low probability. The NOAA Fisheries concluded that implementation of the proposed actions will adversely affect, but not likely jeopardize, the continued existence of the sperm whale; leatherback, green, hawksbill, Kemp's ridley, and loggerhead sea turtles; and the Gulf sturgeon.

April 30—May 2, 2002

The MMS held public hearings in Houston, Texas; New Orleans, Louisiana; and Mobile, Alabama, to receive comments on the multisale EIS for CPA Lease Sales 185, 190, 194, 198, and 201, and WPA Lease Sales 187, 192, 196, and 200. One person attended the Houston hearing, but no comments were presented. Seven people attended the New Orleans hearing. Three individuals presented comments, which are summarized in **Chapter 5.5.** of the multisale EIS. There were no attendees at the Mobile hearing.

November 2002

The MMS completed and filed the Final EIS for CPA Lease Sales 185, 190, 194, 198, and 201, and WPA Lease Sales 187, 192, 196, and 200 (multisale EIS) with USEPA. The MMS revised the document using information presented at the hearings and as a result of comments received on the Draft EIS (See **Chapter 5.7.** of the multisale EIS for a complete discussion of comments and responses.).

CPA Lease Sale 194 EA Process

June 4, 2004   The MMS published a Notice of Preparation of an EA on proposed Lease Sale 194. In the notice, MMS requested interested parties to submit comments regarding any new information or issues that should be addressed in the EA. No comments were received.

6.   REFERENCES

Bedell, C. 2004. Post-storm spill response mobilization in Louisiana. In: Proceedings, Twenty-second Information Transfer Meeting, January 2003. U.S. Dept of the Interior, Minerals Management Service, Gulf of Mexico OCS Region, New Orleans, LA. OCS Study MMS 2003-073. 98 pp.

Dimarco, S.F., M.K. Howard, W.D. Nowlin, Jr., and R.O. Reid. 2004. Subsurface, high-speed current jets in the deepwater region of the Gulf of Mexico. U.S. Dept. of the Interior, Minerals Management Service, Gulf of Mexico OCS Region, New Orleans, LA. OCS Study MMS 2004-022. 98 pp.

Geraci, J.R. and D.J. St. Aubin. 1980. Offshore petroleum resource development and marine mammals: A review and research recommendations. Marine Fisheries Review 42:1-12.

Greenberg, J. 2004. OSV day rates. Workboat 61(7): 10, July.

Hamilton, P., J.J. Singer, E. Waddell, and K. Donahue. 2003. Deepwater observations in the Northern Gulf of Mexico from in-situ current meters and PIES: Final report. Volume II: Technical report. U.S. Dept of the Interior, Minerals Management Service, Gulf of Mexico OCS Region, New Orleans, LA. OCS Study MMS 2003-049. 95 pp.

Hemmerling, S.A. and C.E. Colten. 2003. Environmental justice considerations in Lafourche Parish, Louisiana. U.S. Dept. of the Interior, Minerals Management Service, Gulf of Mexico OCS Region, New Orleans, LA. OCS Study MMS 2003-038.

Lore G.L., D.A. Marin, E.C. Batchelder, W.C. Courtwright, R.P. Desselles, and R.J. Klazynski. 2001. 2000 assessment of conventionally recoverable hydrocarbon resources of the Gulf of Mexico and Atlantic Outer Continental Shelf as of January 1, 1999. U.S. Dept. of the Interior, Minerals Management Service, Gulf of Mexico OCS Region, New Orleans, LA. OCS Report MMS 2001-087.

Oilnergy. 2004. Internet website: http://www.oilnergy.com. July 22, 2004.

Pritchard, P.C.H. 1997. Evolution, phylogeny, and current status. In: Lutz, P.L. and Musivk, J. A. eds. The biology of sea turtles. Boca Raton, FL: CRC Press. Pp. 1-28.

U.S. Dept. of Commerce. National Marine Fisheries Service. 2003. Barataria Plaquemines Barrier Island Complex Project, CWPPRA Project Fed. No./BA-38, Pass La Mer to Chaland Pass and Pelican Island Environmental Assessment. U.S. Dept. of Commerce, National Oceanic and Atmospheric Administration, National Marine Fisheries Service, prepared by Tetra Tech EM Inc. Baton Rouge, Louisiana, December, 2003. 89 pp. + apps.

U.S. Dept. of Commerce. National Oceanic and Atmospheric Administration Fisheries. 2004. Draft 2003 stock assessment reports. Internet website: http://www.nmfs.noaa.gov/prot_res/ PR2/Stock_Assessment_Program/sars_draft.html.

U.S. Dept. of the Interior, Fish and Wildlife Service and Gulf States Marine Fisheries Commission. 1995. Gulf sturgeon *(Acipenser oxyrinchus desotoi)* recovery/management plan. Prepared by the Gulf Sturgeon Recovery/Management Task Team for the U.S. Dept. of the Interior, Fish and Wildlife Service, Southeast Region, Atlanta, GA; the Gulf States Marine Fisheries Commission, Ocean Springs, MS; and the U.S. Dept. of Commerce, National Marine Fisheries Service, Washington, DC.

U.S. Dept. of the Interior. Minerals Management Service. 2001. Energy alternatives and the environment. U.S. Dept. of the Interior, Minerals Management Service, Herndon, VA. OCS Report MMS 2001-096.

U.S. Dept. of the Interior. Minerals Management Service. 2002a. Outer continental shelf oil and gas leasing program: 2002-2007—final environmental impact statement; Volumes I and II. U.S. Dept. of the Interior, Minerals Management Service, Washington, DC. OCS EIS/EA MMS 2002-006.

U.S. Dept. of the Interior. Minerals Management Service. 2002b. Gulf of Mexico OCS oil and gas lease sales: 2003-2005; Central Planning Area Sales 185, 190, 194, 198, and 201; Western Planning Area Sales 187, 192, 196, and 200—final environmental impact statement; Volumes I and II. U.S. Dept. of the Interior, Minerals Management Service, Gulf of Mexico OCS Region, New Orleans, LA. OCS EIS/EA MMS 2002-052.

U.S. Dept. of the Interior. Minerals Management Service. 2002c. News Release: MMS preliminary report finds most facilities withstood Hurricane Lili; 6 platforms out of 800 with severe damage; MMS buoy provides important data. U.S. Dept. of the Interior, Minerals Management Service, Gulf of Mexico OCS Region, New Orleans, LA. October 16, 2002.

U.S. Dept. of the Interior. Minerals Management Service. 2002d. Oil-spill risk analysis: Gulf of Mexico Outer Continental Shelf (OCS) lease sales, Central Planning Area and Western Planning Area, 2003-2007 and Gulfwide OCS Program, 2003-2042. U.S. Dept. of the Interior, Minerals Management Service, Washington, DC. OCS Report MMS 2002-032.

U.S. Dept. of the Interior. Minerals Management Service. 2003a. Outer Continental Shelf oil spill during Hurricane Lili, Ship Shoal Block 119: Responses, fate, and effects. U.S. Dept. of the Interior, Minerals Management Service, Gulf of Mexico OCS Region, New Orleans, LA. OCS Report MMS 2003-039.

U.S. Dept. of the Interior. Minerals Management Service. 2003b. Gulf of Mexico OCS oil and gas lease sales: 2003 and 2005; Eastern Planning Area Sales 189 and 197—final environmental impact statement. U.S. Dept. of the Interior, Minerals Management Service, Gulf of Mexico OCS Region, New Orleans, LA. OCS EIS/EA MMS 2003-020.

U.S. Dept. of the Interior. Minerals Management Service. 2003c. Proposed OCS Lease Sale 190, Central Gulf of Mexico—environmental assessment. U.S. Dept. of the Interior, Minerals Management Service, Gulf of Mexico OCS Region, New Orleans, LA. OCS EIS/EA MMS 2003-066.

U.S. Dept. of the Interior. Minerals Management Service. 2004a. Geological and geophysical exploration for mineral resources on the Gulf of Mexico outer continental shelf; final programmatic environmental assessment. Prepared by Continental Shelf Associates, Inc. for the U.S. Dept. of the Interior, Minerals Management Service, Gulf of Mexico OCS Region, New Orleans, LA. OCS EIS/EA MMS 2004-054.

U.S. Dept. of the Interior. Minerals Management Service. 2004b. Issuance of noncompetitive leases for the use of Outer Continental Shelf sand resources from Ship Shoal, offshore central Louisiana for coastal and barrier island nourishment and hurricane levee construction—environmental assessment. U.S. Dept. of the Interior, Minerals Management Service, Herndon, VA. OCS EIS/EA MMS 2004-059.

U.S. Dept. of the Interior. Minerals Management Service. 2004c. Proposed OCS Lease Sale 192, Western Gulf of Mexico—environmental assessment. U.S. Dept. of the Interior, Minerals Management Service, Gulf of Mexico OCS Region, New Orleans, LA. OCS EIS/EA MMS 2004-007.

Würsig, B., T. Jefferson, and D. Schmidly. 2000. The marine mammals of the Gulf of Mexico. College Station, TX: Texas A&M University Press.

APPENDIX A.   NOTICES TO LESSEES AND OPERATORS (NOVEMBER 2002 — PRESENT)

NTL Number	Effective Date	Title
2002-G12	November 4, 2002	*Revised North American Datum 83 Implementation Plan for the Gulf of Mexico*
2002-N13	November 1, 2002	*Drilling and Well Permit and Reporting Forms*
2002-G15	December 20, 2002	*Coastal Zone Management Program Requirements for OCS ROW Pipeline Applications*
2003-G03	January 23, 2003	*Remotely Operated Vehicle Surveys in Deepwater*
2003-G05	February 15, 2003	*Procedures for Submission, Inspection and Selection of Geophysical Data and Information Collected Under a Permit and Processed or Reprocessed by a Permittee or a Third Party*
2003-G02	March 3, 2003	*Ultimate Recovery Abandonment and Bypassing of Zones*
2003-N03	March 7, 2003	*Performance Measures for OCS Operators and Form MMS-131*
2003-N04	May 9, 2003	*Extension of Lease Terms by Production in Paying Quantities*
2003-N06	June 17, 2003	*Supplemental Bond Procedures*
2003-G10	June 19, 2003	*Vessel Strike Avoidance and Injured/Dead Protected Species Reporting*
2003-G11	June 19, 2003	*Marine Trash and Debris Awareness and Elimination*
2003-G15	August 13, 2003	*Contact with District Offices and the Pipeline Section Outside Regular Work Hours*
2003-G16	August 15, 2003	*Assessment of Existing OCS Platforms*
2003-G17	August 27, 2003	*Guidance for Submitting Exploration Plans and Development Operations Coordination Documents*

NTL Number	Effective Date	Title
2003-G19	September 1, 2003	*Drilling Windows, Eastern Gulf of Mexico*
2003-G20	January 1, 2004	*Gas Volume Statement Requirements*
2004-N01	January 12, 2004	*Revised Assessment Matrix*
2004-G02	January 27, 2004	*Military Warning and Water Test Areas*
2004-G03	February 6, 2004	*Notification and Confirmation of Deep Gas Royalty Relief*
2004-G01	March 1, 2004	*Implementation of Seismic Survey Mitigation Measures and Protected Species Observer Program*
2004-G04	March 7, 2004	*Standard Reporting Period for the Well Activity Report*
2004-G05	April 1, 2004	*Biologically Sensitive Areas of the Gulf of Mexico*
2004-G06	April 5, 2004	*Structure Removal Operations*
2004-G07	April 20, 2004	*Well Records Submittal*
2004-G08	April 21, 2004	*Flaring and Venting Approval Guidelines*
2004-G11	May 3, 2004	*Clarification of Deep Gas Royalty Relief Regulation Regarding Natural Gas Liquids and Pipeline (Retrograde) Condensate*
2004-G09	May 17, 2004	*Policies for Shutting-In Producible Wells During Rig Moves*
2004-G10	June 1, 2004	*Implementation of the eWell Permitting and Reporting System*
2004-G07 Addendum 1	June 1, 2004	*Change of MMS Contractor Receiving Digital Well Log Drilling Records and Additional Well Log Curves to Submit*
2004-N03	July 26, 2004	*Directional and Inclination Survey Data Submission Requirements*
2004-G12	June 21, 2004	*Clarification of Deep Gas Royalty Suspension Provision in Lease Instrument Relating to Sidetrack Completions*

NTL Number	Effective Date	Title
2004-G13	June 22, 2004	*Replacing Deep Gas Royalty Relief Provisions in Lease Instrument With Regulatory Deep Gas Royalty Relief Provisions*
2004-G14	June 23, 2004	*Hurricane and Tropical Storm Evacuation and Production Curtailment Statistics*
2004-N04	June 25, 2004	*Data and Information to be Made Available to the Public*
2004-G15	August 10, 2004	*Application of the Deep Gas Royalty Relief Rule to Leases Issued from 2001 through 2003*

APPENDIX B.   PUBLICATIONS OF THE ENVIRONMENTAL STUDIES PROGRAM, GULF OF MEXICO OCS REGION (NOVEMBER 2002 — PRESENT)

Study Number	Title
2002-055	*Northeastern Gulf of Mexico Chemical Oceanography and Hydrography Study, Synthesis Report*
2002-063	*Deepwater Program: Northern Gulf of Mexico Continental Slope Habitats and Benthic Ecology; Year 2: Interim Report*
2002-064	*Lagrangian Study of Circulation, Transport, and Vertical Exchange in the Gulf of Mexico*
2002-072	*Effect of the Oil and Gas Industry on Commuting and Migration Patterns in Louisiana: 1960-1990*
2002-073	*Emissions Inventories of OCS Production and Development Activities in the Gulf of Mexico, Final Report*
2002-077	*Offshore Petroleum Platforms: Functional Significance for Larval Fish Across Longitudinal and Latitudinal Gradients*
2002-078	*Deepwater Program: Bluewater Fishing and OCS Activity, Interactions Between the Fishing and Petroleum Industries in Deepwaters of the Gulf of Mexico, Final Report*
2003-004	*Dynamics of the Oil and Gas Industry in the Gulf of Mexico: 1980-2000, Final Report*
2003-005	*Proceedings: Twenty-first Annual Gulf of Mexico Information Transfer Meeting, January 2002*
2003-009	*Rigs and Reefs: A Comparison of the Fish Communities at Two Artificial Reefs, a Production Platform, and a Natural Reef in the Northern Gulf of Mexico; Final Report*
2003-018	*Modeling the Economic Impacts of Offshore Oil and Gas Activities in the Gulf of Mexico: Methods and Applications*
2003-022	*Labor Demand in the Offshore Oil and Gas Industry in the 1990's: The Louisiana Case*
2003-029	*Importance of Zooplankton in the Diets of Blue Runner (Caranx crysos) Near Offshore Petroleum Platforms in the Northern Gulf of Mexico*

Study Number	Title
2003-030	*Workshop on Deepwater Environmental Studies Strategy: A Five-Year Follow-Up and Planning for the Future; May 29-31, 2002*
2003-031	*Long-Term Monitoring at the East and West Flower Garden Banks National Marine Sanctuary, 1998-2001; Final Report*
2003-038	*Environmental Justice Considerations in Lafourche Parish, Louisiana*
2003-040	*Marine and Coastal Fishes Subject to Impingement by Cooling-Water Intake Systems in the Northern Gulf of Mexico: An Annotated Bibliography*
2003-041	*Changing Patterns of Ownership and Control in the Petroleum Industry: Implications on the Market for Oil and Gas Leases in the Gulf of Mexico OCS Region, 1983-1999*
2003-048 2003-049	*Deepwater Observations in the Northern Gulf of Mexico from In-situ Current Meters and PIES* *Volume I: Executive Summary* *Volume II: Technical Report*
2003-060 2003-061 2003-062	*Refining and Revising the Gulf of Mexico Outer Continental Shelf Region High-Probability Model for Historic Shipwrecks, Final Report* *Volume I: Executive Summary* *Volume II: Technical Narrative* *Volume III: Appendices*
2003-063	*Historical Reconstruction of the Contaminant Loading and Biological Responses in the Central Gulf of Mexico Shelf Sediments*
2003-065	*Preparation of an Interactive Key for Northern Gulf of Mexico Polychaete Taxonomy Employing the DELTA/INTKEY System, FInal Report*
2003-069	*Sperm Whale Seismic Study in the Gulf of Mexico, Annual Report: Year 1*
2003-072	*Selected Aspects of the Ecology of the Continental Slope Fauna of the Gulf of Mexico: A Synopsis of the Northern Gulf of Mexico Continental Slope Study, 1983-1988*
2003-073	*Proceedings: Twenty-Second Annual Gulf of Mexico Information Transfer Meeting, January 2003*
2003-074	*Modeling and Data Analyses of Circulation Processes in the Gulf of Mexico, Final Report*

Study Number	Title
2004-009	*Long-Term Oil and Gas Structure Installation and Removal Forecasting in the Gulf of Mexico: A Decision- and Resource-Based Approach*
2004-013	*Intermediate Depth Circulation in the Gulf of Mexico: PALACE Float Results for the Gulf of Mexico Between April 1998 and March 2002*
2004-015	*Minerals Management Service Environmental Studies Program: A History of Biological Investigations in the Gulf of Mexico, 1973-2000*
2004-016	*Fiscal System Analysis: Concessionary and Contractual Systems Used in Offshore Petroleum Arrangements*
2004-017	*Cross-Shelf Exchange Processes and the Deepwater Circulation of the Gulf of Mexico: Dynamical Effects of Submarine Canyons and Interactions of Loop Current Eddies with Topography, Final Report*
2004-022	*Subsurface, High-Speed Current Jets in the Deepwater Region of the Gulf of Mexico, Final Report*
2004-027	*Deepwater Program: OCS-Related Infrastructure in the Gulf of Mexico Fact Book*
2004-040	*Strong Mid-Depth Currents and a Deep Cyclonic Gyre in the Gulf of Mexico*
2004-041	*Economic Impact in the U.S. of Deepwater Projects: A Survey of Five Projects*
2004-047	*Supply Network for Deepwater Oil and Gas Development in the Gulf of Mexico: An Empirical Analysis of Demand for Port Services, Final Report*

2004-049
2004-050
 	
2004-051
	History of the Offshore Oil and Gas Industry in Southern Louisiana: Interim Report
	    Volume I: Papers on the Evolving Offshore Industry
	    Volume II: Bayou Lafourche — An Oral History of the Development of the Oil and Gas Industry
	    Volume III: Samples of Interviews and Ethnographic Preferences

2004-057	*Labor Migration and the Deepwater Oil Industry*

The Department of the Interior Mission

As the Nation's principal conservation agency, the Department of the Interior has responsibility for most of our nationally owned public lands and natural resources. This includes fostering sound use of our land and water resources; protecting our fish, wildlife, and biological diversity; preserving the environmental and cultural values of our national parks and historical places; and providing for the enjoyment of life through outdoor recreation. The Department assesses our energy and mineral resources and works to ensure that their development is in the best interests of all our people by encouraging stewardship and citizen participation in their care. The Department also has a major responsibility for American Indian reservation communities and for people who live in island territories under U.S. administration.

The Minerals Management Service Mission

As a bureau of the Department of the Interior, the Minerals Management Service's (MMS) primary responsibilities are to manage the mineral resources located on the Nation's Outer Continental Shelf (OCS), collect revenue from the Federal OCS and onshore Federal and Indian lands, and distribute those revenues.

Moreover, in working to meet its responsibilities, the **Offshore Minerals Management Program** administers the OCS competitive leasing program and oversees the safe and environmentally sound exploration and production of our Nation's offshore natural gas, oil and other mineral resources. The MMS **Minerals Revenue Management** meets its responsibilities by ensuring the efficient, timely and accurate collection and disbursement of revenue from mineral leasing and production due to Indian tribes and allottees, States and the U.S. Treasury.

The MMS strives to fulfill its responsibilities through the general guiding principles of: (1) being responsive to the public's concerns and interests by maintaining a dialogue with all potentially affected parties and (2) carrying out its programs with an emphasis on working to enhance the quality of life for all Americans by lending MMS assistance and expertise to economic development and environmental protection.

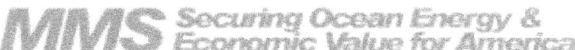